The Future Revolution
of
Transforming Business
Through Sustainable Innovation

Written By

Istiaque Mahmud

Mesbah Uddin

Md. Firoz Hossain

Md Omar Farouk

Tahmina Ali Adrita

Nayem Roshan Jeet

Maniruzzaman Bhuiyan

Mohammad Iftekhar Ashik Imran

Author's Opinion

The Future Revolution of Transforming Business Through Sustainable Innovation" has been an enriching journey. As the lead author, I have had the honor of collaborating with an outstanding team to explore the critical role of sustainable innovation in reshaping business practices. This book examines how forward-thinking companies integrate sustainability not as an afterthought but as the core of their operations. We provide actionable insights into how businesses can innovate to address environmental and social challenges while fostering long-term economic growth. By blending theory with practical examples, we've inspired business leaders and entrepreneurs to embrace change and lead the charge in the sustainability revolution. This book will serve as a roadmap for future business practices and as a catalyst for those seeking to drive real impact in a rapidly evolving world.

- Istiaque Mahmud

Our book covers various emerging technologies that will impact various sectors. We've presented each innovation clearly, highlighting how they will affect industries and everyday life. It's an informative and exciting guide for anyone interested in the future of technology, and I believe it will inspire readers to think critically about the world of tomorrow. In Chapter 10, we investigate the use of environmentally friendly technology in electronic manufacturing, including renewable energy and circular economy techniques. These observations provide readers with a glimpse into the ways in which individuals and corporations can take the lead in transitioning to environmentally friendly technological solutions. I have no doubt that this book will prove to be an invaluable resource for everyone who is interested in comprehending and adjusting to a future that incorporates sustainability.

- Mesbah Uddin

Contributing to 'Future Tech: 20 Innovations That Will Change Our World' has been an enriching experience. Our book dives into transformative technologies, explaining their significance in shaping tomorrow's world. We've explored a wide range of innovations, from AI to biotechnology, presenting them in a manner that is both informative and accessible. Our goal is to make readers aware of these technologies' immense potential for the future. I am proud to be part of this project and confident it will be a valuable resource for anyone interested in future tech. Chapter 7 addresses green hospital designs and energy-efficient healthcare systems, emphasising actionable measures industry may implement to attain sustainability. We have elucidated these principles to render them approachable and actionable for readers. I take pride in having contributed to a book that both informs and enables individuals and organisations to adopt sustainable ideas.

- **Md. Firoz Hossain**

The book sheds light on groundbreaking technologies shaping future industries, economies, and societies. We've carefully researched each innovation to provide clear, engaging insights into their potential impact. It's a forward-looking guide for anyone interested in the evolution of technology. I'm excited about this book's possibilities, and I hope it inspires readers to embrace the future with curiosity and optimism. Chapter 13 examined themes such as resource optimisation and lean manufacturing, demonstrating how industries might diminish their environmental impact while maintaining efficiency. The content demonstrates the equilibrium between technical progress and environmental stewardship, offering a framework for forward-thinking industrial practices. I aspire for this chapter, and the book overall, to motivate readers to adopt expansive perspectives on sustainability within their own domains.

- **Md Omar Farouk**

Collaborating on 'Future Tech: 20 Innovations That Will Change Our World' has been exciting and enlightening. This book explores revolutionary innovations set to redefine the way we live and work. We have focused on clearly understanding each technology, making it accessible to readers of all backgrounds. These advancements are shaping the world of tomorrow, and I believe our book will help readers prepare for and embrace these changes. It's a must-read for anyone eager to understand the technological future. Chapter 19 explores regenerative farming and precision agriculture, highlighting their significance in maintaining global food security and conserving biodiversity. These subjects illustrate the convergence of technology and sustainable practices in tackling significant difficulties. I contend that this book serves as a conduit linking readers to the prospects of a more sustainable and intelligent future.

- **Tahmina Ali Adrita**

This book captures emerging technologies' essence and potential to transform our future. We've taken complex innovations and broken them down in a way that's easy to understand, making the book accessible to both tech enthusiasts and novices. It's exciting to be part of a project highlighting innovations poised to revolutionize industries and our daily lives. I believe this book will inspire readers to engage with the future of technology. Chapter 11 examines the impact of AI and machine learning on sustainability initiatives, including supply chain optimization and energy efficiency enhancement. The book conveys these transformative ideas as approachable insights, encouraging readers to imagine a future in which technology catalyzes sustainable advancement. This initiative has enhanced my comprehension of how innovation can facilitate significant change, and I aspire for readers to find it similarly motivating.

- **Nayem Roshan Jeet**

We offer insights into innovations impacting everything from healthcare to communication. We've simplified complex technologies to ensure that every reader, regardless of expertise, can grasp their significance. I believe this book will guide those eager to explore the future and understand the trends that will shape our world. Chapter 20 examines technologies such as climate-resilient crops and intelligent irrigation, illustrating how agriculture can sustainably prosper through technological progress. By deconstructing these concepts, we intend to render the future of agriculture palpable and engaging for readers. This book serves as a manual for understanding and accepting the continually changing realms of technology and sustainability.

- Maniruzzaman Bhuiyan

Writing The Future Revolution of Transforming Business Through Sustainable Innovation has been a deeply inspiring experience. This book reflects our conviction that the future of business depends on the ability to innovate sustainably—balancing economic success with environmental stewardship and social responsibility. Throughout our research, we discovered countless examples of companies that are pioneering bold new approaches, proving that sustainable innovation is not only viable but essential for lasting success. Our goal is to equip readers with practical frameworks and visionary ideas that encourage them to rethink their business models and lead meaningful change. We believe that embracing sustainability today is the key to unlocking new markets, strengthening communities, and securing a prosperous future for generations to come. This book is a call to action for anyone committed to driving innovation that truly matters.

- Mohammad Iftekhar Ashik Imran

Table of Contents

Introduction 15

CHAPTER 1 16

Introduction to Sustainable Innovation in Business 16

    Understanding the Core Principles of Sustainable Innovation 16

    Importance of Integrating Innovation with Sustainability Goals 17

    Evolution of Sustainability-Driven Business Models 17

    Role of Technology and Eco-Friendly Designs in Driving Innovation 18

    Global Demand for Businesses to Adopt Sustainable Practices 19

    Corporate Responsibility in Fostering Sustainable Transformation 19

CHAPTER 2 20

The Role of Innovation in Business Growth 20

    Linking Innovation to Long-Term Business Growth and Resilience 21

    Creating Competitive Advantages Through Innovative Practices 21

    Role of Research and Development in Sustainability 22

    Building a Culture of Sustainability-Driven Innovation 22

    Real-World Examples of Businesses Scaling Through Innovation 22

    Future Trends in Sustainability and Business Models 23

CHAPTER 3 24

Challenges and Opportunities in Sustainable Innovation 24

    Common Barriers to Adopting Sustainable Practices 24

    Opportunities Presented by Green Markets and Consumer Demand 25

    Leveraging Government Incentives and Policies 25

    The Role of Innovation in Navigating Sustainability Regulations 26

    Strategic Advantages of Integrating Sustainability into Business Models 26

    Case Studies of Successful Navigation of Challenges 27

CHAPTER 4 28

Sustainable Innovation in the Educational Industry 28

    Importance of Embedding Sustainability into Educational Frameworks 28

    Campus-Wide Practices for Reducing Environmental Impact 29

Benefits of Green Infrastructure and Design in Schools 30

Role of Educational Institutions in Shaping Sustainable Leaders 31

Global Initiatives Promoting Sustainability in Education 31

Case Studies of Successful Green Educational Practices 32

CHAPTER 5 33

Innovations in Educational Tools and Technologies 33

Advancements in Sustainable Digital Learning Platforms 33

Integration of Renewable Energy Technologies in Campuses 34

Smart Technologies Improving Educational Efficiency 35

E-Learning's Role in Reducing Education's Carbon Footprint 35

Role of Virtual Reality and AI in Sustainable Education 35

Examples of Green Tech Adoption in Global Institutions 36

CHAPTER 6 37

Building Sustainable Knowledge and Mindsets 37

Developing Sustainability-Focused Leadership Skills in Students 38

Creating Industry Partnerships to Promote Sustainable Knowledge 38

Role of Hands-On Projects in Embedding Sustainability Values 39

Curriculum Reform to Include Sustainability in Core Subjects 39

Training Future Professionals for Sustainability Challenges 40

Best Practices in Fostering Eco-Conscious Mindsets 41

CHAPTER 7 42

Sustainable Practices in Healthcare Systems 42

Green Hospital Designs and Energy-Efficient Healthcare Operations 43

Reducing Carbon Footprints in Healthcare Supply Chains 44

Implementing Renewable Energy in Healthcare Facilities 44

Sustainable Waste Management and Medical Packaging 44

Promoting Eco-Friendly Practices in Patient Care Delivery 45

Case Studies of Hospitals Leading Sustainable Healthcare 46

CHAPTER 8 47

The Role of Innovation in Healthcare Sustainability 47

Technological Innovations Reducing Environmental Impact in Healthcare 47

Advancements in Telemedicine and Its Sustainability Benefits 48

AI Applications for Sustainable Healthcare Management 49

Innovations in Green Pharmaceuticals and Biotechnology 50

Zero-Waste Initiatives in Healthcare Systems 50

Success Stories of Sustainable Practices in Healthcare Innovation 51

CHAPTER 9 52

Ethical Healthcare Innovations 52

Ensuring Equitable Access to Sustainable Healthcare Solutions 53

Public-Private Partnerships Driving Ethical Innovations 53

Leveraging Technology to Address Healthcare Inequalities 54

Affordable Access to Green Medical Technologies.. 54

Global Collaboration for Advancing Sustainable Healthcare Equity 55

Examples of Innovative Solutions Benefiting Underserved Populations............... 56

CHAPTER 10 57

Green Technologies and Innovations 57

Role of Renewable Energy in Powering Tech Infrastructure.................................. 58

Circular Economy Practices in Electronic Manufacturing 58

Innovations in Reducing Electronic Waste (E-Waste) 58

Using AI to Optimize Energy Efficiency in Tech Systems 59

Case Studies of Tech Companies Adopting Green Innovations 60

Emerging Trends in Eco-Friendly Product Design 60

CHAPTER 11 62

Implementation of ML and AI in Business 62

The Transformative Role of AI and ML in Sustainability....................................... 63

Enhancing Supply Chain Efficiency Through AI-Driven Analytics...................... 63

AI Applications in Optimizing Energy Consumption 63

Machine Learning for Predictive Resource Management 64

Leveraging AI for Personalized, Sustainable Consumer Experiences................... 64

Case Studies of Businesses Excelling with AI-Driven Sustainability 65

CHAPTER 12 66

Data Science, Market Innovation, and the Future of Tech Startups 66

Role of Data Science in Sustainable Market Analysis 66

Innovations in Product Design Based on Consumer Sustainability Insights 67

Startups Leveraging AI and Blockchain for Sustainability 67

Scaling Eco-Friendly Innovations with Funding and Accelerators 68

Data-Driven Strategies for Reducing Carbon Footprints 68

Future Trends in Sustainable Tech Startup Ecosystems 68

CHAPTER 13 70

Introduction to Sustainable Industrial Engineering 70

Principles of Resource Optimization and Waste Reduction in Engineering 71

Role of Eco-Design in Reducing Industrial Environmental Impact 72

Lean Manufacturing and Circular Economy Principles 72

Innovations in Sustainable Materials and Energy-Efficient Systems 73

Designing for Recyclability and Longevity in Industrial Products 74

Success Stories of Businesses Adopting Sustainable Engineering Practices 74

CHAPTER 14 75

Life Cycle Assessment (LCA) and Its Role in Industrial Engineering 75

Understanding the Phases and Importance of LCA in Industry 75

Benefits of LCA for Identifying Environmental Impact Hotspots 76

Tools and Software Enabling LCA in Industrial Processes 77

Integrating LCA into Supply Chain Evaluation 77

Future Advancements in AI-Driven LCA Techniques 78

CHAPTER 15 80

Raising Awareness and Building Skills for Sustainable Practices 80

Designing Sustainability-Focused Training Programs for Engineers 81

Developing Skills for Implementing LCA in Industrial Operations 81

Collaborative Efforts Between Academia and Industry for Awareness 82

Leadership's Role in Fostering a Culture of Sustainability 83

Best Practices in Promoting Sustainable Engineering Mindsets 83

Strategies for Driving Industry-Wide Adoption of Eco-Conscious Practices 84

CHAPTER 16 86

Transition to Renewable Energy 86

Importance of Renewable Energy in Reducing Global Emissions 86

Advancements in Solar, Wind, and Hydro Technologies 87

Business Models for Renewable Energy Integration 88

Case Studies of Successful Renewable Energy Transitions 89

Government Incentives and Policies Driving Renewable Adoption 90

Future Trends in Renewable Energy Storage and Grid Technologies 90

CHAPTER 17 92

Smart Grids and Energy Storage 92

Role of Smart Grids in Optimizing Energy Distribution 93

Demand-Response Systems for Energy Efficiency 93

Innovations in Battery Storage Solutions 94

Benefits of Decentralized Energy Systems for Businesses 94

Case Studies of Cities Implementing Smart Grids 95

Future Advancements in Energy Storage and Grid Management 96

CHAPTER 18 98

Circular Economy in Energy 98

Principles of Circular Economy in Energy Production 99

Waste-to-Energy Innovations Reducing Energy Wastage 99

Closed-Loop Energy Systems in Industrial Operations 100

Role of AI in Managing Circular Energy Models 101

Examples of Businesses Benefiting from Circular Energy Practices 101

Policies Promoting Circular Energy Initiatives Globally 102

CHAPTER 19 103

Sustainable Farming Practices 103

Importance of Regenerative Farming for Soil Health and Biodiversity 104

Role of Precision Agriculture in Reducing Resource Waste 104

Transitioning to Organic Farming and Eco-Friendly Pest Control 105

Leveraging Renewable Energy in Farming Operations 106

Case Studies of Farms Achieving Sustainability Goals 107

Future of Farming: Innovations for Global Food Security 107

CHAPTER 20 109

Technological Innovations in Agriculture 109

    Role of AI and IoT in Optimizing Farming Efficiency 109

    Smart Irrigation and Water Conservation Technologies 110

    Advancements in Climate-Resilient Crop Development 111

    Robotics and Automation in Sustainable Agriculture 112

    Blockchain for Transparent and Sustainable Food Supply Chains 113

    Emerging Trends in Vertical and Urban Farming Innovations 113

CHAPTER 21 115

Sustainable Food Systems and Global Challenges 115

    Challenges of Global Hunger and Food Insecurity 115

    Reducing Food Waste Through Circular Economy Practices 116

    Developing Sustainable Food Supply Chains and Logistics 117

    118

    Integrating Eco-Friendly Packaging in Food Distribution 118

    Policies and Partnerships Promoting Sustainable Food Systems 119

    Case Studies of Impactful Sustainable Food Initiatives 120

Summary 121

Conclusion 124

Introduction

The world is constantly changing, and businesses need to adapt as well. Now it is not a web, sustainability is the cloth itself and you must make everything out of this material. The world over, companies are finding that sustainability can be a proxy for eco-friendly technology and show the path to environmental conservation too. For a company that used to sound like a pipe dream, adaptations of this kind are close to becoming present reality and symbolize the future for businesses — those who can sustainably grow with sustainable practices shall last.

In the years ahead, a revolution in how business operates and innovates is at work. Rising from green energy to AI-based sustainable solutions, sustainability needs to be deeply rooted in business models...the way industries breathe, across all sectors—be it healthcare or tech; manufacturing, and agriculture. The Future Revolution of Transforming Business Through Sustainable Innovation™ is the title of a book through which companies can also learn to become leaders in innovation transformation. We will explore what these changes are, and how companies can innovate more responsibly, consuming less refuse with scarce resources and modern technologies created to establish a very sustainable future.

In Entropic, you will discover how to put AI, data science & industrial engineering to work for your business while saving the planet in the process. Real Examples: we will cover actual examples from the real world, ethical perspectives, and business-related challenges in moving to a more sustainable business format. Ready to see if innovation can drive your business forward and be sustainable? Well, we will dive into what the future of business looks like today.

CHAPTER 1

Introduction to Sustainable Innovation in Business

Sustainable innovation is not merely a buzzword but a paradigm shifts redefining how businesses operate in a rapidly changing world. It combines the principles of innovation with the pressing need to address environmental, social, and economic challenges, creating a balanced approach to progress. Sustainable innovation empowers companies to transcend traditional profit-focused models, steering toward long-term value creation for society, the planet, and their stakeholders. In a world grappling with climate change, resource scarcity, and social inequality, the integration of sustainability and innovation is no longer optional—it is essential for survival and growth. This chapter provides a comprehensive overview of sustainable innovation, exploring its evolution, fundamental principles, and the pivotal role it plays in reshaping industries to align with the global movement toward sustainability. Understanding this concept is critical for any organization aiming to lead in a future defined by responsible progress.

Understanding the Core Principles of Sustainable Innovation

At its essence, sustainable innovation integrates environmental stewardship, economic growth, and social responsibility, forming the foundation of a triple bottom line. Unlike conventional innovation, which often prioritizes short-term gains, sustainable innovation takes a long-term perspective, addressing systemic issues such as climate change, inequality, and resource depletion. Businesses embracing this approach rethink their processes, products, and services, designing them to minimize waste, reduce carbon footprints, and deliver benefits to society. For example, adopting renewable materials, implementing circular supply chains, and fostering inclusive workforce practices are manifestations of these principles. By aligning profitability with purpose, sustainable innovation ensures resilience and adaptability in volatile markets, creating a win-win scenario where both business and society thrive.

Importance of Integrating Innovation with Sustainability Goals

Integrating sustainability goals with innovation is a game-changing strategy that transforms how businesses operate, grow, and impact the world. This integration enables companies to future-proof their operations, aligning with evolving consumer preferences and stricter environmental

regulations. Businesses that proactively innovate toward sustainability enjoy significant advantages, from accessing green financing and tax incentives to opening new markets for eco-conscious products and services. Moreover, such alignment fosters a purpose-driven culture within organizations, motivating employees to contribute meaningfully to global challenges. This approach also mitigates risks, such as supply chain disruptions caused by climate-related events, while unlocking new growth opportunities. By making sustainability an integral part of their innovation strategy, companies can position themselves as industry leaders committed to shaping a sustainable future.

Evolution of Sustainability-Driven Business Models

The journey of sustainability-driven business models reflects the growing realization that profitability and responsibility can coexist. In the past, businesses treated sustainability as a compliance requirement or a peripheral concern. However, with increasing consumer awareness, technological advancements, and global environmental challenges, sustainability has become central to competitive strategy. Circular economy models, for instance, have emerged as transformative frameworks where waste is treated as a resource, creating closed-loop systems. Renewable energy integration and zero-waste manufacturing processes are further examples of this evolution. These models emphasize creating shared value, ensuring that business operations benefit not just shareholders but also communities and ecosystems. Companies adopting these models gain a reputation for innovation and leadership, positioning themselves at the forefront of a sustainable future.

Role of Technology and Eco-Friendly Designs in Driving Innovation

Technology is the driving force behind sustainable innovation, offering businesses the tools to rethink operations, reduce waste, and improve efficiency. Breakthroughs in artificial intelligence, blockchain, and the Internet of Things (IoT) enable smarter supply chains, precise

resource management, and transparent sustainability practices. For instance, IoT sensors monitor energy consumption in real-time, allowing companies to minimize waste and lower costs.

Meanwhile, eco-friendly designs focus on reducing environmental impact throughout a product's lifecycle, from material sourcing to disposal. Examples include biodegradable packaging, energy-efficient devices, and modular products that can be repaired or upgraded. By harnessing technology and prioritizing sustainable design, businesses can innovate responsibly while meeting customer demands for environmentally conscious solutions.

Global Demand for Businesses to Adopt Sustainable Practices

An unprecedented combination of environmental, regulatory, and consumer pressures drives the demand for sustainable business practices. Climate change, resource depletion, and pollution have escalated the urgency for corporate accountability. Governments worldwide are implementing policies and incentives to encourage businesses to adopt sustainable practices, such as carbon taxes, green subsidies, and stricter environmental compliance laws. Simultaneously, consumers are becoming more discerning, favoring brands that align with their values and demonstrate genuine commitment to sustainability. This shift has created immense opportunities for businesses to innovate and differentiate themselves in competitive markets. Companies that embrace sustainability not only gain a loyal customer base but also contribute to shaping a global economy rooted in environmental and social responsibility.

Corporate Responsibility in Fostering Sustainable Transformation

Corporate responsibility is a fundamental driver of sustainable transformation, urging businesses to move beyond profit maximization to address broader societal and environmental challenges. Responsible corporations adopt practices such as transitioning to renewable energy, investing in fair trade supply chains, and supporting community development initiatives. These efforts enhance trust and goodwill among stakeholders, strengthening brand reputation and fostering long-term loyalty. Moreover, corporate responsibility inspires a culture of innovation, encouraging employees to develop creative solutions for sustainability challenges. By leading with integrity and purpose, businesses can catalyze industry-wide changes, creating a ripple effect that promotes sustainability across entire sectors. In doing so, they lay the groundwork for a future where businesses are not just contributors to economic growth but also stewards of the planet.

CHAPTER 2

The Role of Innovation in Business Growth

Innovation is the lifeblood of business growth, driving progress, competitiveness, and adaptability in ever-changing markets. In the current era, innovation that incorporates sustainability principles has emerged as a critical factor in ensuring long-term success. Companies that invest in sustainable innovation are better equipped to address evolving consumer expectations, regulatory demands, and environmental risks. Beyond survival, these businesses thrive by discovering new revenue streams, enhancing operational efficiency, and fostering resilience against market disruptions. This chapter explores the multifaceted role of innovation in business growth, focusing on how it contributes to resilience, creates competitive advantages, and lays the foundation for sustainable business models. Through real-world examples, it highlights the transformative potential of integrating innovation with sustainability.

Linking Innovation to Long-Term Business Growth and Resilience

Sustainable innovation is not just about solving immediate challenges—it is about building a foundation for long-term growth and resilience. Businesses that invest in innovation to address resource constraints, climate risks, and social disparities position themselves to weather future uncertainties. For instance, companies that adopt renewable energy solutions or optimize water usage are less vulnerable to fluctuations in resource availability or regulatory changes. Moreover, sustainable innovation opens new avenues for growth by aligning with global trends such as decarburization and digital transformation. By embracing this approach, businesses ensure their survival and their ability to thrive in a dynamic and unpredictable future.

Creating Competitive Advantages Through Innovative Practices

Innovative practices provide businesses with a significant edge, particularly in markets where sustainability is becoming a competitive differentiator. By adopting green technologies, reducing carbon footprints, or offering eco-friendly products, companies can cater to the growing segment of environmentally conscious consumers. These practices enhance brand reputation and

attract investors seeking socially responsible opportunities. Additionally, businesses that lead in sustainable innovation set industry standards, positioning themselves as thought leaders and innovators. This competitive advantage is amplified as sustainability becomes a key criterion for partnerships, government contracts, and customer loyalty in global markets.

Role of Research and Development in Sustainability

Research and development (R&D) serve as the engine driving sustainable innovation, enabling businesses to explore groundbreaking solutions to complex challenges. Through R&D, companies can develop new materials, processes, and technologies that reduce environmental impact and improve efficiency. For instance, advancements in biodegradable plastics, renewable energy storage, and precision agriculture are products of intensive R&D efforts. By prioritizing sustainability in their research agendas, businesses can unlock opportunities for differentiation, cost savings, and market expansion. Moreover, sustained investment in R&D positions companies to stay ahead of regulatory trends and consumer expectations, ensuring their continued relevance and success.

Building a Culture of Sustainability-Driven Innovation

Creating a culture of sustainability-driven innovation requires businesses to embed sustainability into their organizational DNA. This involves not only setting ambitious environmental goals but also fostering an environment that encourages creativity and collaboration. Leadership plays a crucial role by prioritizing sustainability initiatives and empowering employees at all levels to contribute innovative ideas. Employee training programs, cross-functional teams, and partnerships with external stakeholders can further enhance this culture. When sustainability becomes a core organizational value, businesses are better positioned to innovate solutions that address pressing challenges while driving long-term growth and impact.

Real-World Examples of Businesses Scaling Through Innovation

Numerous companies illustrate the transformative power of sustainable innovation. Tesla revolutionized the automotive industry with electric vehicles and renewable energy solutions, demonstrating the potential for disruptive innovation to reshape markets. Similarly, Unilever integrated sustainability into its supply chain, achieving cost efficiencies while reducing environmental impact. These examples showcase how businesses can scale through innovation, aligning profitability with responsibility. By taking bold, proactive steps, these companies not only meet their sustainability goals but also influence their industries to follow suit, creating a ripple effect of positive change.

Future Trends in Sustainability and Business Models

The future of business innovation lies in embracing sustainability as a strategic imperative. Trends such as circular economy adoption, renewable energy integration, and advanced AI-driven solutions are reshaping industries. Companies that anticipate these shifts and adapt accordingly position themselves for sustained success. Additionally, emerging technologies like blockchain and IoT offer new opportunities to enhance transparency, reduce waste, and optimize operations. Businesses that invest in these future trends will not only remain competitive but also play a pivotal role in shaping a sustainable global economy.

CHAPTER 3

Challenges and Opportunities in Sustainable Innovation

Sustainable innovation, while promising transformative potential, is not without its challenges. Businesses face numerous obstacles in aligning innovation with sustainability, ranging from financial constraints to resistance to change within organizational cultures. These barriers often deter companies from fully committing to sustainable practices, even as global demands for environmental responsibility intensify. At the same time, the opportunities presented by sustainable innovation far outweigh the challenges. The rise of green markets, government incentives, and consumer preference for sustainable products provides a fertile ground for businesses to thrive. This chapter explores the key barriers to adopting sustainable innovation identifies opportunities for businesses to leverage sustainability as a growth driver, and examines how policies and regulations influence the sustainability landscape.

Common Barriers to Adopting Sustainable Practices

While there is no question that implementing sustainable practices is beneficial, there are also substantial hurdles that firms must face. The high initial investments required for environmentally friendly technology, such as renewable energy systems or biodegradable materials, are a deterrent for many businesses, many of which are small and medium-sized businesses. One such obstacle that frequently arises is reluctance to change within an organization. This is because existing workflows and priorities frequently come into conflict with sustainability aims. The complexity of creating sustainable supply chains, which requires coordinated efforts across various stakeholders, is another challenge that must be overcome. Additionally, businesses struggle with the dilemma of balancing the benefits of long-term sustainability with the short-term profitability of their operations. In light of these problems, it is clear that robust strategies and support mechanisms are required in order to enable businesses to overcome obstacles and make the shift towards sustainable innovation.

Opportunities Presented by Green Markets and Consumer Demand

The global shift toward eco-conscious living has created unparalleled opportunities for businesses that embrace sustainable innovation. Green markets are expanding rapidly, driven by consumer preferences for environmentally friendly products and services. Companies that align their offerings with these demands can capture significant market share and build enduring customer loyalty. For instance, the rise of plant-based foods, electric vehicles, and energy-efficient appliances illustrates how sustainable innovation is reshaping industries. Moreover, businesses that pioneer in green markets benefit from first-mover advantages, setting industry benchmarks and influencing consumer expectations. These opportunities underscore the importance of anticipating and responding to emerging sustainability trends.

Leveraging Government Incentives and Policies

Governments around the world are introducing policies and incentives to encourage sustainable business practices, presenting a valuable opportunity for innovation. Subsidies for renewable energy adoption, tax breaks for eco-friendly operations, and grants for research into sustainable technologies are just a few examples of support mechanisms available to businesses. These policies not only reduce the financial burden of sustainability initiatives but also create a competitive advantage for companies that comply early. Additionally, businesses that align with international environmental standards, such as carbon neutrality goals or sustainable development targets, position themselves as global leaders. Understanding and leveraging these incentives is essential for companies aiming to thrive in a sustainability-focused economy.

The Role of Innovation in Navigating Sustainability Regulations

Innovation plays a critical role in helping businesses navigate the complexities of sustainability regulations. From emissions controls to waste management mandates, evolving regulatory frameworks often challenge traditional business models. However, companies that adopt innovative approaches can turn compliance into a competitive advantage. For example, AI-powered monitoring systems can ensure real-time compliance with environmental standards, while blockchain technology can enhance supply chain transparency. These innovations not only simplify regulatory adherence but also improve operational efficiency and brand reputation. Businesses that proactively innovate to align with regulations can transform compliance into an opportunity for growth and differentiation.

Strategic Advantages of Integrating Sustainability into Business Models

The incorporation of sustainability into fundamental business models provides substantial advantages from a strategic standpoint. Investors are more likely to be interested in businesses that include sustainability into their operations. This is especially true in light of the fact that ESG (environmental, social, and governance) factors are becoming increasingly important in the financial markets. Additionally, sustainable firms strengthen their resistance to environmental and market disturbances, which ensures that they will continue to be profitable over the long term. Furthermore, aligning with sustainability goals builds relationships with stakeholders, including as consumers, employees, and communities, which in turn fosters trust and loyalty among those stakeholders. Businesses not only achieve their ethical responsibilities when they make sustainability a cornerstone of their plans, but they also ensure a competitive edge in a world that is becoming increasingly environmentally sensitive about the environment.

Case Studies of Successful Navigation of Challenges

Numerous companies have successfully overcome challenges in adopting sustainable innovation, offering valuable lessons for others. For instance, Patagonia has demonstrated how prioritizing environmental responsibility can drive profitability and brand loyalty. Through its

commitment to sustainable supply chains and eco-friendly product designs, the company has set a benchmark in the retail industry. Similarly, Tesla's bold investment in electric vehicle technology overcame initial skepticism to revolutionize the automotive market. These examples highlight the transformative potential of perseverance and innovation in overcoming barriers and turning sustainability challenges into opportunities for growth and impact.

CHAPTER 4

Sustainable Innovation in the Educational Industry

Educational institutions play a crucial role in shaping the future, and as such, they bear significant responsibility for fostering sustainability in their operations, curricula, and policies. Schools, colleges, and universities are uniquely positioned to influence societal attitudes, empowering the next generation to become stewards of environmental and social well-being. By adopting sustainable practices, institutions not only reduce their environmental footprints but also demonstrate leadership in addressing global challenges. From implementing green campus initiatives to incorporating sustainability into educational frameworks, the transition toward sustainable education is essential for cultivating eco-conscious mindsets. This chapter delves into the critical aspects of sustainability in educational institutions, exploring best practices, the benefits of green infrastructure, and the importance of integrating sustainability into both operations and learning environments.

Importance of Embedding Sustainability into Educational Frameworks

Sustainability in education goes beyond infrastructure improvements; it involves embedding sustainability principles into the institutional ethos and pedagogical frameworks. By integrating environmental and social consciousness into curricula, schools, and universities cultivate a generation that values eco-friendly practices and understands the importance of sustainable development. This process often includes offering specialized courses on sustainability, incorporating practical projects that address real-world environmental challenges, and engaging students in active discussions about the consequences of unsustainable behaviors. Moreover, when educational frameworks embrace sustainability, they inspire innovation and critical thinking among students, encouraging them to devise creative solutions for pressing global issues. By fostering such an environment, institutions help build a future workforce that prioritizes ethical decision-making and long-term impacts over short-term gains.

Campus-Wide Practices for Reducing Environmental Impact

Green campus initiatives are pivotal in reducing environmental footprints and fostering sustainability within educational institutions. These practices range from energy-efficient lighting and solar panel installations to waste reduction programs and water conservation systems. Schools and universities can adopt renewable energy sources to power their operations while implementing efficient waste management strategies, such as composting and recycling programs, to minimize landfill contributions. Encouraging alternative transportation methods, like cycling or carpooling, reduces emissions associated with commuting. These efforts reduce operational costs and serve as visible, real-life examples of sustainable practices for students and staff, reinforcing the importance of ecological responsibility. Over time, these campus-wide initiatives can transform educational institutions into sustainability champions, setting benchmarks for other sectors to follow.

Benefits of Green Infrastructure and Design in Schools

Green infrastructure and sustainable design have far-reaching benefits for educational institutions, extending beyond environmental advantages. Features such as energy-efficient buildings, improved ventilation systems, and natural lighting enhance the learning environment, fostering better health and academic performance among students. By utilizing renewable materials and energy sources, institutions significantly reduce their carbon footprints and operational expenses. Moreover, green infrastructure often includes outdoor learning spaces and eco-friendly designs that connect students with nature, encouraging an appreciation for the environment. These designs align with broader sustainability goals, serving as both functional spaces and educational tools. When students learn and engage in settings that embody sustainable principles, they are more likely to internalize and replicate these practices in their personal and professional lives.

Role of Educational Institutions in Shaping Sustainable Leaders

Educational institutions hold the unique power to shape the leaders of tomorrow by equipping students with the knowledge, skills, and values necessary to address global sustainability challenges. By offering leadership programs focused on sustainability, institutions prepare students to take on roles in government, business, and civil society with an eco-conscious mindset. Collaborative projects, internships with sustainability-focused organizations, and exposure to cutting-edge green technologies further enhance their preparedness. Beyond academics, schools, and universities can foster leadership by involving students in campus sustainability initiatives, empowering them to lead projects and campaigns. This hands-on experience not only builds critical skills but also instills a deep sense of responsibility, encouraging students to champion sustainability in their future careers.

Global Initiatives Promoting Sustainability in Education

Numerous global initiatives have been launched to integrate sustainability into education, reinforcing its importance on a worldwide scale. Programs like UNESCO's Education for

Sustainable Development (ESD) emphasize the need to equip learners with the knowledge and skills to drive societal transformation. Similarly, initiatives like the Green School Alliance and LEED certifications for green campuses promote sustainable practices in schools and universities. These programs provide frameworks and resources that help institutions adopt sustainability measures, from implementing energy-efficient infrastructure to developing eco-focused curricula. By participating in these global initiatives, educational institutions align themselves with international sustainability standards, gaining recognition as leaders in the movement for a greener future. Such collaborations also create opportunities for resource sharing and partnerships, amplifying their impact.

Case Studies of Successful Green Educational Practices

Several educational institutions have demonstrated exceptional leadership in integrating sustainability into their operations and curricula, serving as models for others. For example, Green Mountain College in Vermont was one of the first institutions to achieve carbon neutrality through renewable energy projects, efficiency measures, and educational programs centered on sustainability. Similarly, the University of British Columbia incorporates green technologies into its infrastructure, such as geothermal heating and rainwater harvesting systems, while also offering courses that prioritize environmental responsibility. These case studies highlight the potential for educational institutions to lead by example, inspiring their communities to adopt sustainable practices and emphasizing the importance of aligning education with ecological and societal goals.

CHAPTER 5

Innovations in Educational Tools and Technologies

Technology has revolutionized education, offering innovative tools and methods to enhance learning experiences while promoting sustainability. From virtual classrooms to smart technologies that optimize energy use, education systems worldwide are embracing digital transformation to reduce their environmental footprints. Sustainable innovations in educational tools not only lower resource consumption but also make learning more accessible and efficient. These technologies enable schools and universities to adopt greener practices, such as reducing paper waste through e-learning platforms or utilizing AI for resource management. The convergence of technology and sustainability in education is investigated in this chapter. Particular attention is paid to digital learning, the incorporation of environmentally friendly technology, and case studies of educational institutions that are utilising innovation to generate sustainable outcomes.

Advancements in Sustainable Digital Learning Platforms

The advent of digital learning platforms has brought about a revolution in education by providing a more environmentally friendly alternative to the conventional teaching techniques. Because they do away with the requirement for traditional textbooks, paper handouts, and huge classroom rooms, e-learning platforms drastically cut down on the amount of resources that are consumed. Furthermore, virtual classrooms and online courses broaden access to education, making it possible for students living in remote places to benefit from academic opportunities without incurring the environmental costs associated with transportation. Additionally, these platforms offer the possibility of personalized learning experiences, which make use of adaptive technologies to suit to the specific requirements of each individual. It is possible for educational institutions to promote sustainability while simultaneously ensuring that students receive a high-quality education that is suited to their specific needs if they utilize digital learning platforms.

Integration of Renewable Energy Technologies in Campuses

The integration of renewable energy technologies, such as solar panels, wind turbines, and geothermal systems, is transforming campuses into models of sustainability. These systems not only reduce the reliance on fossil fuels but also serve as hands-on educational tools for students studying renewable energy and environmental science. For instance, many universities have implemented solar farms to power their operations, significantly reducing their carbon footprints while saving on energy costs. Beyond infrastructure, renewable energy projects often involve students and faculty in research and development, fostering innovation and a deeper understanding of sustainability. Such initiatives demonstrate the dual benefit of reducing environmental impact while enhancing educational opportunities.

Smart Technologies Improving Educational Efficiency

Smart technologies, including IoT-enabled devices and AI-driven systems, are revolutionizing how educational institutions manage resources. These technologies enable real-time monitoring of energy use, water consumption, and waste management, allowing campuses to optimize efficiency and minimize costs. For example, smart HVAC systems automatically adjust heating and cooling based on occupancy, significantly reducing energy wastage. Similarly, AI-powered scheduling tools ensure efficient use of classroom spaces and other facilities. By leveraging smart technologies, educational institutions can not only achieve sustainability goals but also provide students with a firsthand experience of innovative solutions that address environmental challenges.

E-Learning's Role in Reducing Education's Carbon Footprint

E-learning platforms are instrumental in reducing the carbon footprint of education by eliminating the need for printed materials and physical transportation. With the rise of virtual classrooms and online degree programs, students and educators can connect from anywhere in the world, reducing the environmental impact associated with traditional education models. Additionally, these platforms enable institutions to expand their reach to underserved populations without increasing infrastructure demands. By adopting e-learning solutions, schools and universities contribute to sustainability while ensuring that education remains accessible, inclusive, and effective for all learners.

Role of Virtual Reality and AI in Sustainable Education

Virtual reality (VR) and artificial intelligence (AI) are opening new frontiers in sustainable education by offering immersive learning experiences with minimal resource use. VR allows students to explore complex subjects, such as environmental science or architecture, in virtual environments without the need for physical materials or field trips. AI, on the other hand, personalizes learning experiences, enabling institutions to identify and address individual student needs more effectively. Together, these technologies create opportunities for innovation in teaching and learning while promoting sustainability through reduced resource consumption and enhanced accessibility.

Examples of Green Tech Adoption in Global Institutions

Educational institutions worldwide are leveraging green technologies to align with sustainability goals. For instance, Stanford University has implemented a state-of-the-art energy management system that integrates renewable energy sources with efficient cooling and heating technologies. Similarly, Singapore's Nanyang Technological University has developed a fully self-sustaining eco-campus featuring green buildings, smart technologies, and extensive renewable energy systems. These examples showcase how institutions can adopt innovative technologies to achieve sustainability milestones while providing students with a cutting-edge learning environment. By leading in green tech adoption, these institutions inspire others to follow suit and contribute to global sustainability efforts.

CHAPTER 6

Building Sustainable Knowledge and Mindsets

Education is the foundation upon which sustainable futures are built. As the global economy transitions toward sustainability, equipping students with the necessary skills and mindsets to address complex environmental challenges becomes critical. This chapter delves into the transformative role of educational institutions in fostering sustainability-focused leadership and innovation. It explores the strategies educators can adopt to instill eco-conscious values and practical skills in students. Through hands-on projects, curriculum reforms, and collaborations with industries, educational frameworks can bridge the gap between academic knowledge and real-world sustainability practices. This chapter also highlights the necessity of rethinking traditional education systems to prepare students for the environmental, social, and economic challenges of tomorrow. By integrating sustainability into the core ethos of education, institutions can mold future leaders who are not only well-informed but also deeply committed to driving positive change. Real-life case studies and best practices will serve as benchmarks to illustrate the profound impact of sustainable education on students and society.

Developing Sustainability-Focused Leadership Skills in Students

Leadership rooted in sustainability is vital for tackling global environmental and social challenges. Educators play a pivotal role in shaping this leadership by embedding sustainability into learning objectives and extracurricular initiatives. Students must learn to think critically about the interplay between human activities and environmental impacts, fostering a sense of responsibility. Programs such as student-led green projects and leadership workshops can be instrumental. These initiatives encourage collaborative problem-solving, innovation, and the application of sustainable practices. For instance, creating mock environmental policies or participating in community green audits allows students to practice real-world decision-making. As future leaders, students need exposure to scenarios that demand ethical and sustainable choices, helping them internalize these values. Schools that prioritize leadership development through sustainable lenses cultivate individuals ready to spearhead transformative change. Education systems can prepare students to balance economic progress with ecological preservation in their future careers by fostering a mindset where leadership aligns with sustainability.

Creating Industry Partnerships to Promote Sustainable Knowledge

Partnerships between educational institutions and industries are instrumental in advancing sustainability knowledge. Industry collaborations offer students firsthand exposure to cutting-edge

sustainability practices while giving businesses access to fresh perspectives from future leaders. These partnerships can manifest as internships, mentorships, or joint research projects focusing on sustainability goals. For instance, partnerships with renewable energy firms or eco-friendly manufacturing companies allow students to apply theoretical knowledge to real-world challenges. Moreover, businesses can guide curriculum development to reflect evolving industry needs, ensuring students remain competitive and aligned with market trends. Institutions can also invite industry leaders for guest lectures, workshops, or sustainability-focused seminars to inspire students and offer practical insights. Through these collaborations, students gain invaluable experience while industries benefit from innovative ideas. Ultimately, such partnerships are a symbiotic relationship that accelerates sustainable transformation in education and beyond, creating a workforce equipped to address the demands of a greener future.

Role of Hands-On Projects in Embedding Sustainability Values

Experiential learning through hands-on projects is a powerful tool for embedding sustainability values in students. By engaging directly with environmental challenges, students develop a deeper understanding of sustainable practices and their real-world applications. Projects such as designing eco-friendly buildings, conducting waste audits, or creating renewable energy models allow students to translate classroom knowledge into actionable solutions. These activities also foster creativity, teamwork, and problem-solving skills, which are essential for driving sustainable innovation. For instance, schools that incorporate gardening projects or renewable energy installations empower students to witness the tangible impact of their efforts. Furthermore, involving students in local community projects, such as tree planting drives or water conservation programs, helps them connect with their environment while cultivating a sense of stewardship. These hands-on experiences instill lifelong sustainability values, encouraging students to think critically about their actions and their broader impact. By making sustainability practical and engaging, educators can inspire proactive and environmentally conscious citizens.

Curriculum Reform to Include Sustainability in Core Subjects

Reforming academic curricula to integrate sustainability into core subjects is essential for cultivating eco-conscious individuals. While sustainability is often taught as an isolated topic, embedding it across disciplines can provide students with a holistic understanding of its relevance.

For instance, science classes can explore renewable energy technologies, while economics courses examine the financial implications of sustainable practices. Literature courses can analyze environmental themes, and history classes can discuss the impact of human activities on the planet over time. By weaving sustainability into every aspect of education, schools can create a cohesive framework for students to see its importance across all domains. Moreover, interdisciplinary approaches, such as project-based learning, allow students to tackle sustainability challenges using knowledge from multiple subjects. Updating curricula to align with global sustainability standards ensures that students are prepared to meet the demands of an evolving world. This reform is not just an academic shift; it's a crucial step toward building a future-ready society equipped to lead sustainable change.

Training Future Professionals for Sustainability Challenges

To address future sustainability challenges, educational institutions must focus on preparing students to become skilled professionals in green industries. This involves designing programs that emphasize technical expertise in sustainability-related fields, such as renewable energy, green architecture, and sustainable agriculture. Equally important is developing soft skills like collaboration, ethical decision-making, and adaptability, which are critical for navigating complex sustainability challenges. Certification programs, workshops, and field trips to eco-friendly businesses can provide practical exposure, helping students understand industry-specific challenges and solutions. Additionally, offering specialized degrees or elective courses in

sustainability ensures that students interested in these careers receive focused training. Institutions that invest in producing a sustainability-ready workforce not only support global environmental goals but also ensure that their students remain competitive in the job market. By fostering expertise and adaptability, education systems can empower future professionals to drive meaningful change across industries.

Best Practices in Fostering Eco-Conscious Mindsets

Fostering eco-conscious mindsets requires a multi-faceted approach that engages students, educators, and the broader community. Schools can implement practices such as sustainability pledges, green campaigns, or eco-friendly infrastructure to create an environment where sustainability is a shared value. Incorporating mindfulness practices, like nature walks or environmental reflections, can also deepen students' connection to the planet. Additionally, peer-led initiatives, such as green clubs or student ambassador programs, empower young individuals to take ownership of sustainability efforts. Educators play a vital role by modeling eco-conscious behavior, integrating sustainability discussions into lessons, and celebrating student-led achievements. Community involvement, such as partnerships with local environmental organizations or participation in global events like Earth Day, further reinforces these values. By creating a supportive ecosystem, schools can nurture a culture where sustainability is ingrained in every action and decision, inspiring students to adopt eco-conscious habits that last a lifetime.

CHAPTER 7

Sustainable Practices in Healthcare Systems

The healthcare industry stands at a critical juncture where it must balance patient care with environmental responsibility. As one of the most resource-intensive sectors, healthcare operations can significantly impact the planet through energy use, waste production, and resource consumption. Sustainable practices in healthcare systems are essential not only for reducing environmental harm but also for improving operational efficiency and cost-effectiveness. This chapter explores innovative approaches to creating green hospitals, reducing carbon footprints in supply chains, and promoting eco-friendly patient care practices. By adopting renewable energy, sustainable waste management, and advanced technologies, healthcare organizations can lead the way in addressing global sustainability goals. The integration of sustainability into healthcare is more than an ethical choice—it is a strategic necessity that ensures the longevity of both the planet and healthcare services. This chapter also includes case studies of

hospitals that have successfully implemented sustainable practices, showcasing how such initiatives enhance both environmental and patient outcomes.

Green Hospital Designs and Energy-Efficient Healthcare Operations

Green hospitals represent a paradigm shift in healthcare infrastructure, prioritizing energy efficiency and environmental responsibility without compromising patient care. By incorporating elements such as solar panels, green roofs, and advanced HVAC systems, healthcare facilities can significantly reduce their carbon footprints. The use of eco-friendly construction materials and designs that maximize natural lighting further enhances energy efficiency. Beyond infrastructure,

operational strategies, such as adopting energy-efficient medical equipment and implementing strict energy usage protocols, contribute to sustainability. For instance, many hospitals have transitioned to LED lighting and automated energy management systems, which save costs and reduce emissions. These efforts not only align with environmental goals but also improve the overall patient experience by creating healthier, more comfortable environments. Green hospital designs are a testament to the healthcare sector's ability to innovate and lead by example in addressing global sustainability challenges.

Reducing Carbon Footprints in Healthcare Supply Chains

The healthcare supply chain is a significant contributor to the sector's carbon footprint, encompassing everything from procurement to distribution. Streamlining these processes to prioritize sustainability can have far-reaching benefits. Hospitals and clinics can work with suppliers to source eco-friendly products, reduce packaging waste, and optimize logistics to lower transportation emissions. For example, some institutions have adopted digital inventory management systems that minimize overstocking and wastage. Similarly, implementing reusable medical supplies where possible reduces the demand for single-use items that contribute to landfill waste. Collaborative initiatives, such as group purchasing organizations, enable healthcare facilities to leverage economies of scale to secure sustainable products. By addressing inefficiencies and embracing innovative solutions, healthcare organizations can significantly reduce their supply chain's environmental impact, setting a precedent for other industries to follow.

Implementing Renewable Energy in Healthcare Facilities

Renewable energy adoption is a cornerstone of sustainable healthcare practices, offering a clean and reliable alternative to traditional energy sources. Hospitals and clinics, which operate around the clock, require vast amounts of energy, making renewable solutions both an environmental and financial imperative. Solar panels, wind turbines, and geothermal energy systems are increasingly being integrated into healthcare facilities to power operations sustainably. For instance, several hospitals have installed solar arrays to offset their electricity consumption, reducing both emissions and costs. These efforts are often supported by government incentives, grants, and partnerships that make renewable energy transitions more accessible. Beyond environmental benefits, renewable energy also enhances energy resilience, ensuring healthcare services remain uninterrupted during power outages. By investing in renewables, healthcare facilities can lead the charge in building a greener, more sustainable future while maintaining high-quality patient care.

Sustainable Waste Management and Medical Packaging

Effective waste management is a critical component of sustainable healthcare, addressing the sector's substantial production of hazardous and non-hazardous waste. Innovative solutions, such as autoclaving and chemical treatment, allow for the safe disposal of medical waste while minimizing environmental harm. Hospitals can also implement robust recycling programs for non-hazardous materials, such as paper, plastics, and glass. In addition to waste management, rethinking medical packaging is essential for reducing environmental impact. Sustainable packaging options, such as biodegradable materials and reusable containers, are gaining traction as alternatives to traditional, single-use plastics. For example, some healthcare providers now use

refillable medicine dispensers and recyclable blister packs, reducing landfill contributions. Healthcare facilities can significantly lower their ecological footprint by adopting these practices while ensuring compliance with stringent safety standards.

Promoting Eco-Friendly Practices in Patient Care Delivery

Eco-friendly practices in patient care delivery encompass a wide range of initiatives to reduce environmental impact without compromising the quality of care. From telemedicine services that reduce the need for patient travel to using energy-efficient medical devices, healthcare providers are finding innovative ways to enhance sustainability. Additionally, adopting digital record-keeping systems eliminates paper waste, streamlining operations while conserving resources. Hospitals also prioritize using non-toxic cleaning agents and environmentally friendly sterilization methods to create safer, healthier spaces for patients and staff. Furthermore, dietary changes in hospital cafeterias, such as sourcing local, organic foods, contribute to the institution's overall sustainability goals. These efforts highlight how patient care and environmental stewardship can coexist, paving the way for a more sustainable healthcare ecosystem.

Case Studies of Hospitals Leading Sustainable Healthcare

Real-world examples provide valuable insights into the successful implementation of sustainable healthcare practices. One such case is the Dell Children's Medical Center in Texas, which became the first hospital in the world to achieve LEED Platinum certification. Its design incorporates energy-efficient systems, water-saving technologies, and sustainable building materials. Another example is the Karolina University Hospital in Sweden, which uses geothermal energy and advanced waste management systems to minimize its environmental impact. These hospitals demonstrate that sustainability is not only achievable but also beneficial for reducing costs and enhancing patient outcomes. By sharing their strategies and lessons learned, these institutions inspire others in the healthcare sector to adopt similar initiatives, driving collective progress toward a more sustainable future.

CHAPTER 8

The Role of Innovation in Healthcare Sustainability

Innovation is the lifeblood of sustainability in healthcare, driving transformative changes that improve efficiency, reduce environmental impacts, and enhance patient outcomes. From groundbreaking technologies to data-driven solutions, innovation enables healthcare providers to reimagine their operations with a focus on sustainability. This chapter examines how advancements such as AI, telemedicine, and green pharmaceuticals are revolutionizing healthcare practices. By leveraging innovation, healthcare organizations can address pressing challenges such as resource scarcity, waste management, and carbon emissions. The incorporation of cutting-edge technologies not only helps to achieve environmental objectives, but it also helps to increase the resilience and adaptability of healthcare systems. This chapter shows the crucial role that innovation plays in the creation of a sustainable healthcare landscape by utilising success stories and advancements that are at the cutting edge of the field.

Technological Innovations Reducing Environmental Impact in Healthcare

Technological advancements have the potential to transform healthcare into a model of environmental sustainability. From energy-efficient medical devices to smart hospital management systems, these innovations minimize the sector's ecological footprint while enhancing care delivery. For example, IoT (Internet of Things) sensors can optimize resource usages, such as water and electricity, by identifying wasteful patterns in real-time. Similarly, 3D printing technology allows to production of customized medical tools and implants, reducing material waste. Innovations in diagnostic technologies, such as portable imaging devices, further reduce the need for large, energy-intensive equipment. These breakthroughs not only support the healthcare industry's environmental goals but also improve operational efficiency and patient outcomes. By implementing and expanding the use of such technology, healthcare facilities can dramatically lessen their impact on the environment while simultaneously maintaining their position at the forefront of medical innovation.

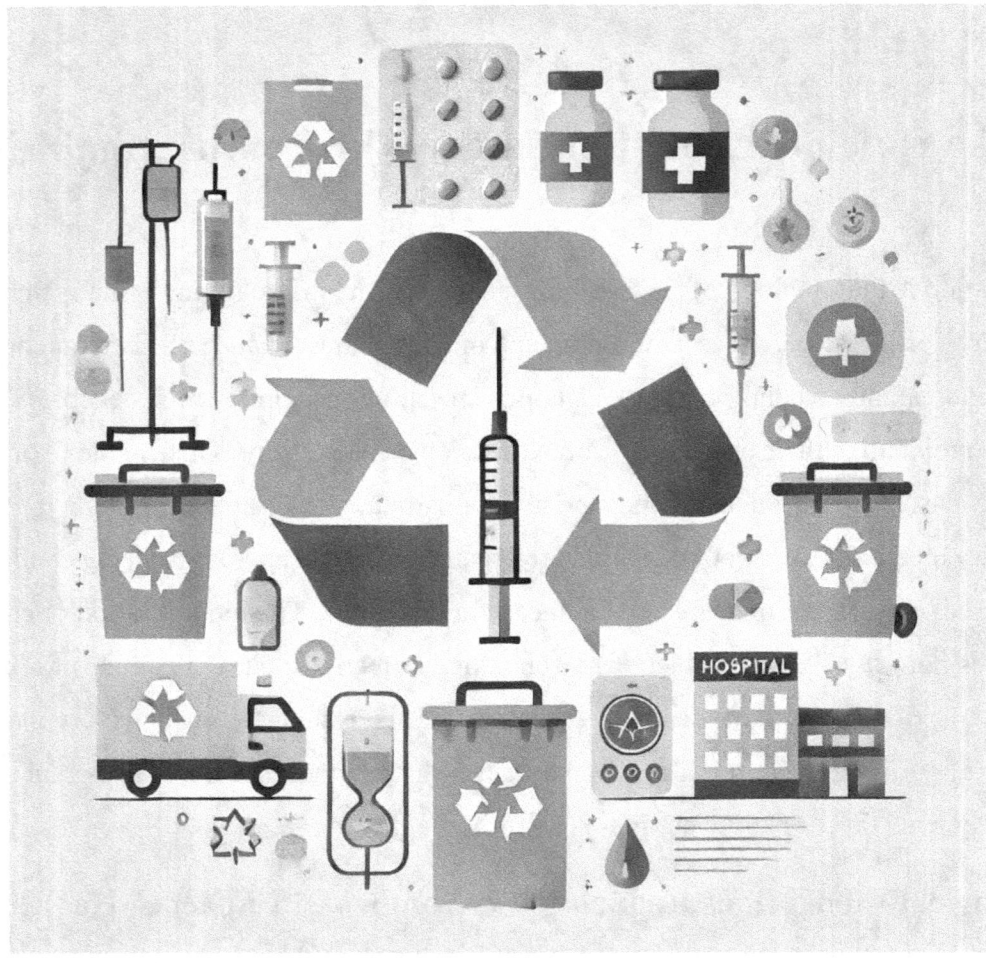

Advancements in Telemedicine and Its Sustainability Benefits

Telemedicine has emerged as a game-changer for both patient care and environmental sustainability. By enabling virtual consultations, telemedicine reduces the need for patient and provider travel, cutting down on greenhouse gas emissions associated with transportation. Additionally, telemedicine minimizes the operational demands of physical facilities, including energy consumption and resource usage. For example, patients in remote areas can access specialized care without the logistical challenges of long-distance travel, making healthcare more equitable and environmentally friendly. Many healthcare providers have also integrated telemedicine platforms with electronic health records (EHR), streamlining administrative processes and reducing paper waste. Beyond convenience, telemedicine's sustainability benefits extend to lowering the sector's overall carbon footprint, creating a win-win scenario for healthcare providers, patients, and the planet.

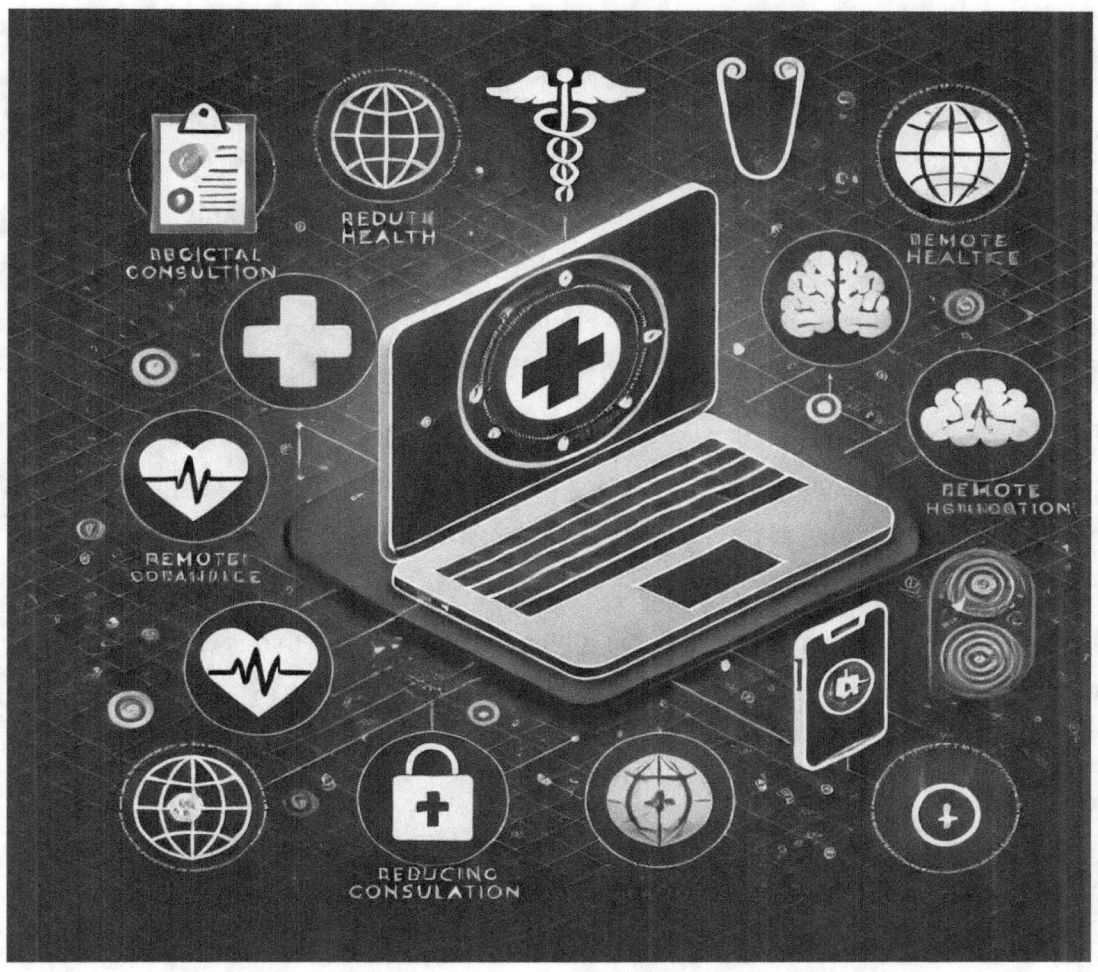

AI Applications for Sustainable Healthcare Management

Artificial intelligence (AI) is revolutionizing sustainable healthcare management by enabling data-driven decision-making and resource optimization. AI-powered tools can analyze vast datasets to identify inefficiencies in hospital operations, such as energy overuse or supply chain bottlenecks. Predictive analytics help healthcare providers anticipate resource needs, preventing overstocking and reducing waste. Additionally, AI-driven systems can optimize patient scheduling and facility management, ensuring minimal energy consumption during off-peak hours. Advanced AI applications in diagnostics and treatment planning also reduce unnecessary medical procedures, conserving resources while improving patient outcomes. For example, AI-based imaging analysis can detect diseases with higher accuracy, reducing the need for repeat tests. As AI continues to evolve, its role in promoting sustainability in healthcare will only grow, offering smarter, greener solutions for complex challenges.

Innovations in Green Pharmaceuticals and Biotechnology

Green pharmaceuticals and biotechnology are transforming drug development and manufacturing with sustainability at the forefront. Traditional pharmaceutical processes often generate significant waste and consume large amounts of energy. Innovations such as biocatalysis and continuous manufacturing are now enabling the production of drugs with fewer environmental impacts. Additionally, researchers are developing biodegradable drug delivery systems that minimize waste and improve patient safety. Biopharmaceuticals derived from renewable resources, such as algae or plant-based compounds, offer sustainable alternatives to synthetic drugs. In addition to the production process, the packaging and distribution of pharmaceuticals are also being rethought to lessen their impact on the environment. The fact that environmental responsibility and innovation are not mutually exclusive is demonstrated by these achievements, which mark a shift towards more sustainable methods in an industry that is essential to the public's health around the world.

Zero-Waste Initiatives in Healthcare Systems

Both the management of resources and the disposal of trash in healthcare systems are being reshaped as a result of zero-waste programs. The elimination of landfill contributions is the primary goal of these programs, which emphasise reducing, reusing, and recycling goods. The first step that hospitals typically take when implementing zero-waste policies is to conduct extensive waste audits in order to identify areas that could use improvement. Examples of initiatives that are becoming normal procedures at progressive healthcare institutions include the use of reusable surgical equipment, the composting of organic waste, and recycling programs for medical plastics. In some institutions, for instance, certain types of medical packaging are now sterilised and reused rather than being thrown away after a single use. The implementation of zero-waste concepts into day-to-day operations not only lessens the impact that healthcare systems have on the environment, but it also reduces the expenses associated with such activities. The adoption of a circular approach to resource management in the healthcare industry is demonstrated by these projects, which indicate both its feasibility and its benefits.

Success Stories of Sustainable Practices in Healthcare Innovation

Several healthcare organizations have set benchmarks in sustainability through innovative practices. One notable example is the Boston Medical Center, which operates on 100% renewable energy and has an on-site farm providing fresh produce for patients and staff. Another success story is Cleveland Clinic, which has implemented energy-efficient HVAC systems, waste reduction initiatives, and water-saving technologies across its campuses. In the pharmaceutical sector, companies like Pfizer have adopted green chemistry principles to minimize waste and energy consumption during drug manufacturing. These organizations showcase how sustainability can be integrated into healthcare at all levels, inspiring others to follow suit. By sharing these success stories, the industry can collectively advance toward a more sustainable future.

CHAPTER 9

Ethical Healthcare Innovations

Ethical healthcare innovations lie at the intersection of sustainability, equity, and technological advancement. As the world grapples with resource scarcity and growing healthcare demands, it is vital to ensure that innovations are not only environmentally responsible but also socially inclusive. This chapter explores how ethical principles guide the development and implementation of sustainable healthcare solutions. From ensuring equitable access to green technologies to fostering global collaborations for healthcare equity, these initiatives address critical gaps in healthcare delivery. The chapter also highlights the role of public-private partnerships and technology in creating affordable, sustainable healthcare options for underserved populations. By placing ethics at the core of innovation, the healthcare sector can drive transformative change that benefits all.

Ensuring Equitable Access to Sustainable Healthcare Solutions

Equitable access to sustainable healthcare solutions is crucial for addressing health disparities while promoting environmental responsibility. Initiatives such as subsidized renewable energy installations for rural clinics and mobile health units powered by green technology are bridging the gap in underserved areas. These solutions ensure that vulnerable populations benefit from sustainable innovations without facing financial barriers. For instance, solar-powered clinics in remote regions not only provide essential medical services but also reduce dependence on fossil fuels. Ensuring equity requires collaborative efforts from governments, NGOs, and private organizations to fund and scale these initiatives. By prioritizing inclusivity, the healthcare industry can ensure that sustainability efforts uplift all communities equally.

Public-Private Partnerships Driving Ethical Innovations

Public-private partnerships (PPPs) are instrumental in driving ethical and sustainable healthcare innovations. These collaborations pool resources, expertise, and funding to tackle complex challenges such as climate change and healthcare accessibility. For example, partnerships between governments and tech companies have led to the development of AI-driven diagnostic

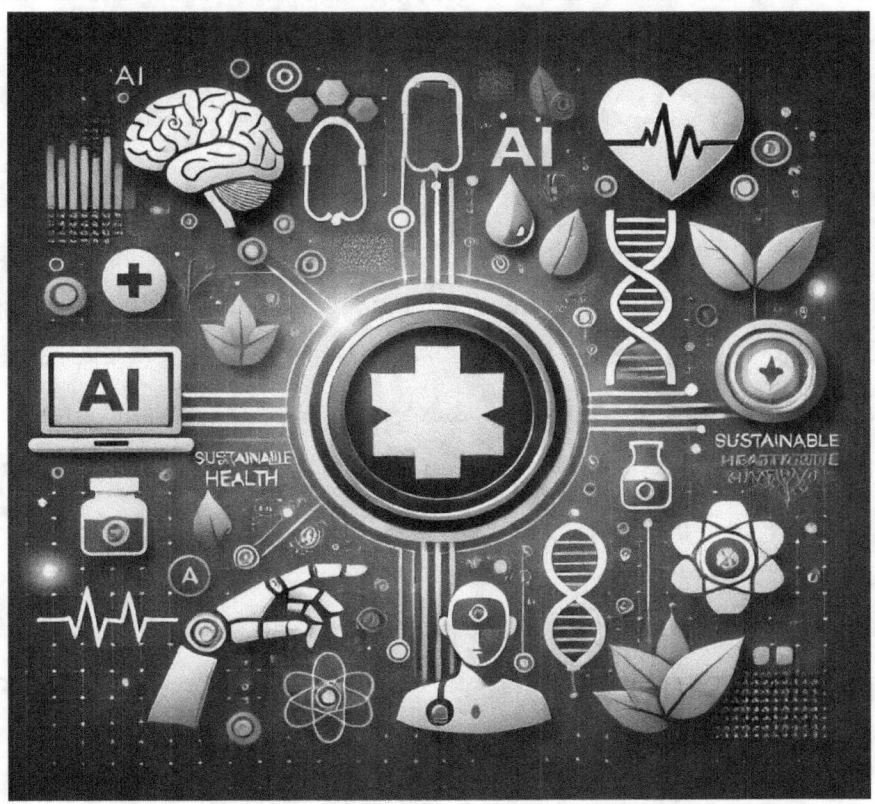

tools for low-resource settings. Similarly, pharmaceutical firms working with non-profits have created affordable green medicines for underprivileged communities. PPPs enable large-scale implementation of sustainable solutions by aligning public interest with private-sector innovation. By fostering trust and shared responsibility, these partnerships amplify the impact of ethical healthcare advancements.

Leveraging Technology to Address Healthcare Inequalities

While simultaneously increasing sustainability, technology is a potent instrument that can be used to alleviate inequities in healthcare provided. Platforms for telehealth, diagnostics driven by artificial intelligence, and mobile health applications are helping to close gaps in the delivery of medical treatment to underprivileged communities. AI systems, for instance, are able to identify high-risk patients in regions that are geographically far, which enables prompt treatments. Individuals are given the ability to take responsibility of their own health through the use of mobile applications that provide educational resources and tools for self-monitoring. The use of these technologies lessens the reliance on physical infrastructure, which in turn reduces both costs and the impact on the environment. Through the utilisation of technology innovation, healthcare practitioners have the ability to develop systems that are more equal and sustainable, thereby benefiting all aspects of society.

Affordable Access to Green Medical Technologies

Making green medical technologies affordable is essential to ensure their widespread adoption, particularly in resource-constrained settings. Many advanced sustainable technologies, such as energy-efficient diagnostic equipment and biodegradable medical products, remain out of reach for low-income regions due to high costs. Governments, non-profits, and private organizations must collaborate to subsidize these innovations, ensuring equitable access. For instance, bulk purchasing agreements or grants can reduce the cost of renewable energy-powered devices for rural clinics. Additionally, designing cost-effective alternatives tailored to local needs, such as solar-powered refrigerators for vaccine storage, can significantly improve healthcare delivery. By addressing affordability, healthcare systems can scale sustainable practices while ensuring that no community is left behind. Affordable access to green medical technologies is a critical step toward creating an inclusive, eco-conscious healthcare ecosystem.

Global Collaboration for Advancing Sustainable Healthcare Equity

Global collaboration is pivotal in advancing both sustainability and equity in healthcare. Organizations like the World Health Organization (WHO) and the United Nations are spearheading initiatives that bring together governments, corporations, and non-profits to address healthcare disparities and environmental challenges simultaneously. For example, international partnerships have funded renewable energy projects for healthcare facilities in underdeveloped regions, ensuring consistent access to essential services. Collaborative platforms also facilitate the exchange of knowledge and resources, allowing countries to adopt proven sustainable practices. Joint research initiatives, such as those focused on developing affordable green pharmaceuticals, exemplify the power of global teamwork. By fostering international collaboration, the healthcare sector can address pressing global issues while paving the way for a more equitable and sustainable future.

Examples of Innovative Solutions Benefiting Underserved Populations

Innovative solutions tailored to underserved populations highlight the intersection of sustainability, technology, and equity. One such example is the deployment of solar-powered clinics in sub-Saharan Africa, where access to electricity is limited. These clinics provide reliable healthcare services while significantly reducing carbon emissions. Another example is the use of mobile health units equipped with telemedicine capabilities in remote Indian villages, allowing residents to consult specialists without the need for travel. Additionally, biodegradable medical supplies, such as compostable syringes, are being introduced in regions with limited waste management infrastructure. These solutions demonstrate how innovation can address both healthcare disparities and environmental challenges, offering scalable models for global adoption. By prioritizing the needs of underserved populations, these initiatives exemplify the transformative potential of sustainable healthcare innovations.

CHAPTER 10

Green Technologies and Innovations

The technology industry plays a dual role in the global sustainability agenda. On one hand, it contributes to environmental challenges through energy-intensive operations and e-waste. On the other, it provides the tools and innovations necessary for driving sustainability across sectors. Green technologies and innovations are at the heart of this transformation, offering eco-friendly alternatives that reduce environmental impacts while enhancing efficiency. This chapter explores key advancements in renewable energy integration,

circular economy practices, and electronic waste reduction. It also highlights how artificial intelligence (AI) is optimizing energy use in tech systems and profiles case studies of companies leading green innovation. By embracing sustainable design and production principles, the technology industry can act as a catalyst for broader ecological and economic change.

Role of Renewable Energy in Powering Tech Infrastructure

The integration of renewable energy into tech infrastructure is a game-changer for reducing the industry's environmental footprint. Data centers, which are critical to modern technology, consume vast amounts of electricity. By transitioning to solar, wind, and hydro energy sources, tech companies can significantly lower their carbon emissions. For example, Google and Microsoft have committed to running their operations entirely on renewable energy, setting benchmarks for the industry. Renewable energy not only mitigates environmental impact but also enhances energy resilience, ensuring uninterrupted operations during grid outages. Moreover, advancements in battery storage technologies are enabling tech facilities to store surplus renewable energy for continuous use. This shift demonstrates the potential of clean energy to power the digital economy sustainably, paving the way for a greener future.

Circular Economy Practices in Electronic Manufacturing

Circular economy practices are redefining electronic manufacturing by focusing on resource efficiency and waste minimization. Unlike the traditional linear model of "take, make, dispose," circular approaches prioritize recycling, reusing, and refurbishing materials. Companies like Apple and Dell are leading this transformation by designing products with modular components that can be easily replaced or upgraded. Additionally, initiatives like e-waste recycling programs recover valuable metals, such as gold and copper, from discarded electronics. These materials are then reintegrated into new products, reducing the demand for virgin resources. Circular practices not only conserve natural resources but also reduce the environmental and social costs associated with mining and disposal. By adopting these principles, the tech industry can establish a sustainable production model that benefits both the planet and consumers.

Innovations in Reducing Electronic Waste (E-Waste)

E-waste represents one of the fastest-growing waste streams globally, posing severe environmental and health risks. Innovations aimed at reducing e-waste are vital for mitigating these challenges. Extended producer responsibility (EPR) programs, where manufacturers take accountability for the lifecycle of their products, have proven effective. Companies are also developing biodegradable electronic components, such as organic circuit boards, which decompose naturally without releasing toxins. Moreover, trade-in and buyback schemes encourage consumers to return old devices for recycling or refurbishment. For example, Samsung's Eco-Exchange program collects outdated devices and ensures their proper disposal or reuse. These innovative strategies are turning the tide on e-waste, showcasing how technological ingenuity can address one of the industry's most pressing challenges.

Using AI to Optimize Energy Efficiency in Tech Systems

Artificial intelligence is revolutionizing energy management in the tech sector by enabling precise and efficient operations. AI-driven algorithms can analyze energy usage patterns in real time, identifying inefficiencies and suggesting optimizations. For instance, AI systems in data centers can dynamically adjust cooling systems based on server activity, reducing energy waste. Similarly, AI tools help optimize manufacturing processes by predicting maintenance needs, preventing downtime, and minimizing energy consumption. Beyond operations, AI applications in smart grids and energy distribution ensure that renewable energy is used efficiently. By harnessing AI, the tech industry is achieving remarkable strides in energy conservation, aligning innovation with environmental goals.

Case Studies of Tech Companies Adopting Green Innovations

Leading tech companies are setting the standard for sustainability through groundbreaking green innovations. For instance, Apple's transition to carbon-neutral operations involves renewable energy investments, eco-friendly product designs, and robust recycling initiatives. Another example is Google's DeepMind AI, which optimizes energy consumption in its data centers, resulting in a 40% reduction in cooling energy usage. Smaller startups are also making an impact, such as Fairphone, which designs modular smartphones with ethically sourced materials. These case studies highlight the diverse ways in which technology companies are embracing sustainability, proving that environmental stewardship and profitability can go hand in hand.

Emerging Trends in Eco-Friendly Product Design

Eco-friendly product design is shaping the future of the tech industry, emphasizing durability, repairability, and environmental responsibility. From energy-efficient appliances to devices made from recycled materials, innovation in product design prioritizes sustainability without compromising performance. For example, HP's EcoSmart printers are designed to use less energy and are manufactured using recycled plastics. Similarly, Google's Nest Thermostat incorporates sustainable materials and features energy-saving algorithms. These trends reflect a growing consumer demand for greener products and a shift in corporate strategies toward long-term sustainability. By investing in eco-friendly designs, tech companies are contributing to a circular economy while meeting the evolving expectations of environmentally conscious consumers.

CHAPTER 11

Implementation of ML and AI in Business

Machine learning (ML) and artificial intelligence (AI) are transforming business operations with unprecedented precision, efficiency, and scalability. These technologies are particularly impactful in promoting sustainability, enabling organizations to optimize resources, reduce waste, and make data-driven decisions. This chapter explores the transformative role of AI and ML in supply chain efficiency, energy optimization, predictive resource management, and personalized consumer experiences. Through case studies and emerging trends, it highlights how businesses are leveraging these tools to align profitability with environmental goals. By integrating AI and ML into their operations, companies are not only enhancing performance but also contributing to a more sustainable future.

The Transformative Role of AI and ML in Sustainability

AI and ML are reshaping sustainability strategies across industries by providing advanced tools for monitoring, analysis, and optimization. For instance, AI-powered analytics help businesses identify inefficiencies in their operations, such as excessive energy use or material waste. These insights enable targeted interventions, reducing costs and environmental impact. In agriculture, ML algorithms optimize irrigation schedules, conserving water while boosting crop yields. Similarly, in logistics, AI systems streamline transportation routes to minimize fuel consumption. By integrating these technologies, businesses can achieve significant sustainability gains, reinforcing the critical role of AI and ML in driving innovation.

Enhancing Supply Chain Efficiency Through AI-Driven Analytics

Supply chains are complex systems with significant environmental and economic implications. AI-driven analytics offer a powerful solution for optimizing these networks, identifying inefficiencies, and reducing waste. Predictive modeling tools can forecast demand accurately, minimizing overproduction and inventory surpluses. Additionally, AI applications in logistics optimize delivery routes, cutting fuel use and emissions. For instance, Amazon uses machine learning to enhance its delivery efficiency, reducing its carbon footprint. By leveraging AI in supply chain management, businesses can achieve cost savings while promoting sustainability throughout their operations.

AI Applications in Optimizing Energy Consumption

AI applications are transforming energy consumption in businesses by enabling smarter, more efficient operations. Through real-time monitoring and adaptive algorithms, AI tools can identify patterns of energy use and suggest actionable changes. For instance, AI-powered systems in manufacturing can dynamically adjust machinery usage based on demand, reducing energy waste. Similarly, in office environments, smart AI solutions control lighting and HVAC systems based on occupancy, cutting unnecessary power usage. The use of AI in renewable energy management is equally transformative; predictive analytics optimize the distribution of solar and wind power to minimize reliance on fossil fuels. By harnessing AI's capabilities, businesses can

significantly lower their energy costs and carbon emissions, aligning their operations with sustainability goals.

Machine Learning for Predictive Resource Management

Predictive resource management powered by machine learning (ML) is enabling businesses to minimize waste and optimize resource utilization. By analyzing historical and real-time data, ML algorithms can anticipate future needs with remarkable accuracy. For example, in agriculture, ML-driven models predict water requirements for crops, reducing over-irrigation and

conserving this vital resource. In manufacturing, predictive tools ensure materials are ordered precisely when needed, avoiding overstock and spoilage. Retailers benefit from inventory optimization, reducing the likelihood of unsold goods going to waste. Predictive resource management not only drives operational efficiency but also strengthens businesses' sustainability practices by reducing their ecological impact.

Leveraging AI for Personalized, Sustainable Consumer Experiences

AI is revolutionizing consumer experiences by tailoring products and services to individual preferences while promoting sustainability. For example, e-commerce platforms use AI to recommend eco-friendly alternatives based on browsing history, encouraging greener purchasing decisions. In the fashion industry, AI tools enable virtual try-ons, reducing returns and the associated carbon footprint. Additionally, AI-powered feedback systems allow businesses to refine their offerings to meet consumer demands for sustainability. These personalized, data-driven approaches not only enhance customer satisfaction but also position businesses as leaders in the shift toward environmentally conscious practices.

Case Studies of Businesses Excelling with AI-Driven Sustainability

Numerous businesses are leveraging AI to advance sustainability while achieving impressive operational gains. For instance, IBM's Watson AI is helping organizations monitor and manage energy usage across facilities, reducing costs and emissions. In logistics, UPS employs AI to optimize delivery routes, saving millions of gallons of fuel annually. Smaller startups are also making an impact; for example, Grid Edge uses AI to optimize energy consumption in buildings. These case studies illustrate how AI-driven solutions can address environmental challenges while delivering tangible business benefits, reinforcing the potential of technology to drive sustainable innovation.

CHAPTER 12

Data Science, Market Innovation, and the Future of Tech Startups

Data science is a cornerstone of sustainable market innovation, providing insights that drive eco-friendly decision-making and operational efficiency. From analyzing consumer behavior to optimizing resource usage, data science empowers businesses to align profitability with sustainability. In the tech startup ecosystem, this intersection of data and innovation is particularly dynamic. Startups are leveraging AI, blockchain, and data-driven strategies to create sustainable solutions, scale eco-friendly products, and secure funding for green technologies. This chapter explores the transformative role of data science in market analysis, innovations in product design, and the emergence of green tech startups. Through case studies and future trends, it highlights how data and technology are shaping a more sustainable and equitable future.

Role of Data Science in Sustainable Market Analysis

Data science enables businesses to understand market trends and consumer behaviors with unprecedented precision, fostering sustainability-driven innovation. By analyzing data on consumer preferences, companies can tailor their products to meet the growing demand for eco-

friendly solutions. For example, supermarkets use data analytics to predict purchasing trends, reducing food waste by optimizing inventory. Similarly, energy providers analyze usage patterns to promote renewable options tailored to customer needs. These insights help businesses create strategies that are both profitable and environmentally responsible, demonstrating the power of data science to drive sustainable market innovation.

Innovations in Product Design Based on Consumer Sustainability Insights

Product design is transforming as businesses use consumer data to inform sustainable innovations. Data analytics reveals preferences for durability, recyclability, and energy efficiency, guiding companies in designing products that align with these values. For instance, automotive manufacturers analyze data to develop electric vehicles with features most desired by eco-conscious buyers. In the tech sector, data-driven insights inform the creation of modular gadgets that reduce electronic waste. By integrating sustainability into the product development lifecycle, companies can meet consumer expectations while contributing to a circular economy.

Startups Leveraging AI and Blockchain for Sustainability

Startups are at the forefront of leveraging AI and blockchain to create innovative solutions for sustainability challenges. AI is helping startups optimize processes such as energy distribution, waste management, and resource allocation. Blockchain, on the other hand, is revolutionizing

supply chain transparency by enabling secure tracking of materials from origin to consumer. For example, startups in the food industry use blockchain to ensure ethical sourcing and reduce food waste. Meanwhile, renewable energy startups utilize AI to forecast energy demand and optimize grid performance. These technologies empower startups to scale their impact, proving that innovation and sustainability can drive entrepreneurial success.

Scaling Eco-Friendly Innovations with Funding and Accelerators

Securing funding and access to accelerators is crucial for startups aiming to scale eco-friendly innovations. Green technology incubators and venture capital firms specializing in sustainability are providing critical support to entrepreneurs. Programs like Clean Energy Ventures and Greentown Labs offer resources, mentorship, and funding to bring sustainable ideas to market. These platforms also connect startups with industry leaders, fostering partnerships that accelerate growth. By aligning their goals with global environmental priorities, startups can attract investors eager to support sustainable solutions, ensuring their innovations reach a broader audience.

Data-Driven Strategies for Reducing Carbon Footprints

Data-driven strategies are empowering businesses to minimize their carbon footprints by identifying and mitigating emissions hotspots. For instance, advanced analytics tools measure the environmental impact of supply chains, guiding companies in adopting greener alternatives. Businesses can also use data to optimize logistics, reduce energy consumption, and transition to renewable energy sources. Predictive models help organizations anticipate and adapt to regulatory changes, ensuring compliance with sustainability standards. By leveraging data, companies can quantify their progress, set achievable goals, and demonstrate their commitment to environmental stewardship.

Future Trends in Sustainable Tech Startup Ecosystems

The future of tech startups is deeply intertwined with sustainability, as emerging trends focus on leveraging advanced technologies for environmental impact. Innovations in vertical farming, renewable energy storage, and zero-waste manufacturing are poised to shape the next generation of startups. Additionally, collaborations between startups and established corporations will drive the adoption of sustainable practices on a larger scale. Technologies such as AI, blockchain, and IoT will continue to play a pivotal role in creating scalable solutions for global challenges. As consumer demand for sustainability grows, the startup ecosystem will become a hub for groundbreaking innovations that prioritize both profit and the planet.

CHAPTER 13

Introduction to Sustainable Industrial Engineering

Industrial engineering is at the forefront of innovation, shaping how resources are utilized, processes are optimized, and products are created. However, as industries expand, the environmental and social impacts of traditional engineering practices become increasingly evident. Sustainable industrial engineering addresses this challenge by integrating eco-friendly principles into every stage of the production cycle. From resource optimization and waste reduction to designing products with recyclability in mind, sustainable industrial engineering is not just about efficiency—it's about creating systems that benefit the planet and society. This chapter explores the core principles of sustainable industrial engineering, highlighting the role of eco-design, lean manufacturing, and energy-efficient systems. By examining real-world examples and success stories, it provides a roadmap for how industries can transition to more sustainable practices without sacrificing innovation or profitability. As the demand for greener solutions grows, sustainable industrial engineering stands as a critical pillar for achieving global environmental goals.

Principles of Resource Optimization and Waste Reduction in Engineering

Resource optimization and waste reduction are cornerstones of sustainable industrial engineering, aiming to maximize efficiency while minimizing environmental impact. Traditional engineering practices often prioritize production speed and cost, inadvertently leading to resource wastage and pollution. In contrast, sustainable approaches focus on using materials, energy, and time as efficiently as possible. Techniques such as value stream mapping and process simulations allow engineers to identify and eliminate inefficiencies in production workflows. Additionally, the adoption of advanced manufacturing technologies, like additive manufacturing, reduces material wastage by enabling precise production. For instance, industries are increasingly turning to 3D

printing to create components with minimal leftover materials. Beyond manufacturing, sustainable waste management systems play a crucial role. Implementing recycling programs, reusing by-products, and converting waste into energy are strategies that align engineering practices with circular economy principles. These methods demonstrate how resource optimization and waste reduction not only benefit the environment but also drive cost savings and operational improvements.

Role of Eco-Design in Reducing Industrial Environmental Impact

Eco-design is a transformative approach that incorporates environmental considerations into product development, emphasizing sustainability without compromising functionality or aesthetics. The process begins with selecting materials that are renewable, recyclable, or biodegradable, reducing the product's ecological footprint from the outset. Eco-design also focuses on minimizing resource use during manufacturing by optimizing product dimensions and employing energy-efficient techniques. For example, lightweight—designing products to use fewer materials without losing strength—has become a common practice in industries such as automotive and packaging. Another critical aspect of eco-design is end-of-life planning, which ensures that products can be disassembled and recycled rather than discarded. Companies like Patagonia exemplify eco-design by creating apparel using recycled materials and offering repair services to extend product life. By integrating eco-design principles, industries can create innovative products that align with consumer demand for sustainability while reducing environmental impact.

Lean Manufacturing and Circular Economy Principles

Lean manufacturing and the circular economy are complementary frameworks that drive sustainability in industrial operations. Lean manufacturing focuses on eliminating waste, improving efficiency, and maximizing value for customers. Techniques such as just-in-time production, where materials are delivered exactly when needed, reduce excess inventory and waste. Lean principles also emphasize continuous improvement, encouraging teams to identify and resolve inefficiencies regularly. When paired with circular economy practices, lean manufacturing becomes even more impactful. The circular economy seeks to design industrial systems that recycle, repurpose, and regenerate resources, effectively closing the loop on waste. For example, industries are increasingly adopting closed-loop systems where waste materials are reintegrated into production. One notable example is the construction sector, where concrete debris is crushed and reused in new projects, reducing the need for virgin materials. By combining lean manufacturing and circular economy principles, industries can achieve unparalleled levels of efficiency and sustainability.

Innovations in Sustainable Materials and Energy-Efficient Systems

Advancements in sustainable materials and energy-efficient systems are revolutionizing industrial engineering, paving the way for greener operations. Sustainable materials, such as bio-based plastics, lightweight composites, and low-carbon concrete, reduce the environmental impact of manufacturing processes while maintaining high performance. For example, companies in the automotive sector are exploring natural fibers and recycled metals to produce lighter, fuel-efficient vehicles. Similarly, energy-efficient systems, such as smart grids, advanced HVAC systems, and energy recovery technologies, minimize energy consumption in industrial facilities. Innovations like regenerative braking systems in machinery capture and reuse energy, enhancing efficiency. The integration of IoT (Internet of Things) devices further optimizes energy usage by providing real-time data on resource consumption, enabling swift adjustments to minimize waste. These innovations not only align industries with sustainability goals but also enhance competitiveness by reducing operating costs and meeting regulatory standards.

Designing for Recyclability and Longevity in Industrial Products

Designing industrial products for recyclability and longevity ensures that resources are used responsibly throughout their lifecycle. Engineers prioritize materials and components that can be easily disassembled, sorted, and recycled, reducing the environmental impact of discarded products. This approach aligns with extended producer responsibility (EPR) policies, which hold manufacturers accountable for the end-of-life management of their products. Designing for longevity is equally important, as it reduces the frequency of replacements and the associated environmental costs. For instance, industries producing consumer electronics are developing modular devices that allow for component upgrades instead of full replacements. Companies like Tesla have embraced this philosophy by designing electric vehicles with batteries that can be refurbished and reused. Such practices not only conserve resources but also resonate with consumers who value durability and sustainability. By designing products for recyclability and longevity, industries can contribute to a circular economy while building trust with environmentally conscious customers.

Success Stories of Businesses Adopting Sustainable Engineering Practices

Several businesses have demonstrated the transformative impact of sustainable industrial engineering through innovative practices. One notable example is Interface, a global carpet manufacturer that has implemented circular economy principles to eliminate waste and reduce emissions. The company sources recycled materials for its products and offers a take-back program to ensure old carpets are repurposed instead of discarded. Another success story is Siemens, which has adopted energy-efficient manufacturing systems across its facilities, achieving significant reductions in energy use and carbon emissions. In the packaging industry, Tetra Pak has introduced renewable and recyclable materials, enabling its products to align with consumer and regulatory demands for sustainability. These businesses highlight how adopting sustainable engineering practices can drive innovation, enhance competitiveness, and contribute to global environmental goals.

CHAPTER 14

Life Cycle Assessment (LCA) and Its Role in Industrial Engineering

L ife Cycle Assessment (LCA) is a powerful tool for understanding and mitigating the environmental impacts of products, services, and processes throughout their life cycles. From raw material extraction and manufacturing to usage and disposal, every stage of a product's journey contributes to its ecological footprint. LCA allows industrial engineers to quantify these impacts, identify hotspots, and implement strategies for improvement. This chapter explores the phases and significance of LCA, highlighting its role in driving sustainability across industries. It also examines the tools and technologies that facilitate LCA, the integration of this assessment into supply chains, and future advancements in AI-driven techniques. Through case studies and practical examples, the chapter illustrates how LCA empowers industries to make data-driven decisions that align with environmental goals and consumer expectations. By adopting LCA practices, organizations can not only enhance sustainability but also gain a competitive edge in an increasingly eco-conscious market.

Understanding the Phases and Importance of LCA in Industry

The Life Cycle Assessment process is divided into four key phases: goal and scope definition, inventory analysis, impact assessment, and interpretation. Each phase provides crucial insights into the environmental footprint of a product or service. The first phase establishes the purpose of the assessment and outlines the boundaries, such as whether the analysis will cover a product's entire lifecycle or specific stages. The inventory analysis phase involves collecting data on resource inputs and emissions and creating a detailed account of environmental impacts. The impact assessment phase evaluates these inputs and emissions against categories like greenhouse gas emissions, water usage, and waste generation. Finally, the interpretation phase synthesizes the findings to identify opportunities for reducing impacts. The importance of LCA lies in its ability to reveal previously overlooked aspects of sustainability. For example, many industries discover that a product's use phase contributes significantly to its overall impact, prompting design improvements for energy efficiency. By addressing these insights, LCA empowers engineers to create more sustainable systems that benefit the environment, consumers, and businesses alike.

Benefits of LCA for Identifying Environmental Impact Hotspots

LCA is invaluable for pinpointing environmental impact hotspots—stages in a product's lifecycle with the greatest ecological burden. Identifying these hotspots enables businesses to prioritize interventions where they matter most. For instance, an LCA of a plastic water bottle might reveal that the production of raw materials, such as polyethylene, accounts for most of its

carbon footprint. This insight allows manufacturers to focus on sourcing recycled materials or developing alternatives. Similarly, in the automotive sector, LCA often highlights the significant emissions generated during vehicle use, driving innovations in fuel efficiency and electrification. Beyond production, LCA can identify inefficiencies in supply chains, such as energy-intensive transportation or wasteful packaging. By targeting these hotspots, companies can implement effective strategies to reduce their environmental footprint and enhance overall sustainability. This proactive approach not only minimizes ecological impacts but also demonstrates corporate responsibility, strengthening a company's reputation in a competitive market.

Tools and Software Enabling LCA in Industrial Processes

Advancements in technology have made LCA more accessible and precise through specialized tools and software. Platforms like GaBi, SimaPro, and OpenLCA provide industrial engineers with comprehensive datasets and user-friendly interfaces for conducting detailed assessments. These tools simplify complex calculations, enabling users to evaluate resource use, emissions, and environmental impacts across different scenarios. Additionally, cloud-based solutions offer collaborative capabilities, allowing teams to share data and insights in real time. Many LCA tools also integrate with existing enterprise systems, such as supply chain management software, to streamline the assessment process. Innovations in AI and machine learning further enhance LCA capabilities by automating data collection and analysis, providing faster and more accurate results. For example, AI-driven algorithms can predict the environmental impact of new designs before they are prototyped, enabling proactive decision-making. By leveraging these tools, businesses can embed sustainability into their operations with greater efficiency and precision, driving meaningful change across industries.

Integrating LCA into Supply Chain Evaluation

The integration of LCA into supply chain evaluation allows businesses to assess and mitigate environmental impacts across their value chains. Supply chains often involve multiple stages and stakeholders, each contributing to the overall ecological footprint of a product. LCA provides a comprehensive view of these interactions, identifying inefficiencies and opportunities for improvement. For example, a food company might use LCA to evaluate the carbon emissions associated with sourcing ingredients, processing, packaging, and transportation. Insights from this analysis could lead to changes such as sourcing from local suppliers, switching to biodegradable packaging, or optimizing logistics routes. Collaboration with suppliers is also crucial for implementing sustainable practices at every stage. Tools like blockchain further enhance LCA integration by ensuring transparency and traceability in supply chains. By incorporating LCA into their supply chain evaluations, businesses can build more sustainable and resilient systems that align with environmental and market demands.

Case Studies Showcasing Effective LCA Implementation

Real-world case studies demonstrate the transformative impact of effective LCA implementation. For example, Unilever conducted an LCA on its detergents and discovered that the product's use phase, particularly energy consumption during washing, had the highest environmental impact. This finding prompted the company to reformulate its products for cold-water washing, significantly reducing emissions. Similarly, in the automotive industry, Tesla employs LCA to analyze the lifecycle impacts of its electric vehicles, from raw material extraction to end-of-life recycling. The insights gained from these assessments guide innovations in battery technology and supply chain optimization. Another notable example is IKEA, which uses LCA to evaluate the sustainability of its furniture, leading to increased use of renewable materials and modular designs for longevity. These case studies highlight how LCA empowers organizations to make informed decisions that drive sustainability while maintaining profitability and customer satisfaction.

Future Advancements in AI-Driven LCA Techniques

The future of LCA lies in harnessing artificial intelligence to enhance accuracy, efficiency, and scalability. AI-driven LCA techniques leverage machine learning algorithms to process vast datasets, identifying patterns and predicting impacts with greater precision. For instance, AI can analyze the environmental performance of materials in real-time, enabling engineers to make sustainable choices during the design phase. Predictive analytics powered by AI can also forecast the long-term impacts of new products, helping businesses align their strategies with sustainability goals. Furthermore, automation simplifies data collection from various sources, such as IoT devices and supply chain systems, reducing the time and effort required for assessments. As AI technologies evolve, they are expected to integrate seamlessly with other digital tools, such as digital twins and blockchain, creating a holistic approach to sustainability management. These advancements will not only make LCA more accessible to businesses of all sizes but also enhance its effectiveness as a cornerstone of sustainable industrial engineering.

CHAPTER 15

Raising Awareness and Building Skills for Sustainable Practices

The transitions to sustainable industrial engineering demands more than technological innovation—it requires a widespread shift in awareness and skill-building within the workforce. Engineers and industry leaders are central to implementing environmentally responsible practices that prioritize resource optimization and waste reduction. However, achieving these goals hinges on fostering a culture that values sustainability at every stage of industrial operations. This chapter focuses on strategies for raising awareness and equipping professionals with the skills necessary to integrate life cycle assessments (LCA) and sustainable principles into industrial processes. From targeted training programs to collaborative efforts between academia and industry, businesses must invest in education and leadership to drive meaningful change. Creating eco-conscious mindsets and embedding sustainability-focused skills are not just ideals; they are essential for staying competitive in a world that demands environmental accountability. This chapter explores best practices, leadership roles, and strategies for fostering awareness, enabling the adoption of sustainable practices across industries.

Designing Sustainability-Focused Training Programs for Engineers

Sustainability-focused training programs are pivotal for ensuring engineers possess the knowledge and expertise to address today's environmental challenges. These programs should integrate both theoretical and practical aspects of sustainable engineering, including resource optimization, waste reduction, and life cycle assessments. Training must focus on equipping professionals with tools and methodologies like LCA software, eco-design principles, and energy-efficient systems. Companies can adopt customized training modules that cater to their specific operational needs while aligning with global environmental standards. Hands-on workshops, simulations, and case studies provide real-world experience, fostering the ability to identify opportunities for sustainability improvements in industrial systems. Partnerships with sustainability-focused organizations and accreditation bodies ensure programs stay up-to-date with emerging trends and practices. By prioritizing sustainability training, businesses can build a workforce capable of driving transformative industrial processes. Ultimately, empowering engineers with these skills positions companies to lead in sustainability and gain a competitive edge in a global market increasingly driven by eco-conscious consumers and regulations.

Developing Skills for Implementing LCA in Industrial Operations

The successful implementation of Life Cycle Assessment (LCA) in industrial operations requires a skilled workforce that can analyze environmental impact across all stages of production. Engineers must develop the technical and analytical abilities to conduct comprehensive LCA evaluations, identify impact hotspots, and propose eco-friendly alternatives. Training should emphasize data analysis, environmental impact modeling, and proficiency with LCA software tools like SimaPro or GaBi. Industries can adopt a multi-tiered skill-building approach by offering foundational courses for new employees and advanced modules for experienced engineers. Collaborating with environmental experts and academia can help organizations provide in-depth insights into cutting-edge LCA techniques. Practical training, such as workshops that simulate real industrial processes, ensures professionals can apply these skills effectively. Furthermore, industries must promote cross-functional collaboration by encouraging engineers to work alongside supply chain managers and sustainability consultants. As companies prioritize LCA implementation, a workforce proficient in these skills becomes an invaluable asset, driving continuous improvement and measurable reductions in environmental impact.

Collaborative Efforts Between Academia and Industry for Awareness

Collaboration between academia and industry is critical to raising awareness about sustainable industrial practices. Universities play a foundational role in educating the next generation of engineers by embedding sustainability principles into curricula, research, and practical training programs. Partnerships between academic institutions and industries create opportunities for students to engage in real-world projects that focus on solving sustainability challenges. Companies can support these initiatives by providing funding, mentorship, and access to operational data for case studies. Internships and apprenticeships allow students to gain hands-on experience, bridging the gap between theory and application. Simultaneously, industries benefit from innovative ideas and research emerging from academic collaboration, driving solutions that optimize resources and reduce environmental footprints. Workshops, industry-sponsored competitions, and joint R&D projects further strengthen this partnership, fostering a shared commitment to sustainability. By investing in these collaborations, businesses ensure a pipeline of skilled professionals who are not only technically proficient but also deeply aware of the need for sustainable industrial operations.

Leadership's Role in Fostering a Culture of Sustainability

Effective leadership is the cornerstone of fostering a culture of sustainability within industries. Leaders set the tone by prioritizing sustainability as a core business objective and ensuring it is integrated into every facet of organizational strategy. To drive this cultural shift, leaders must clearly communicate the importance of sustainability, outlining both its environmental and financial benefits. By setting measurable goals—such as reducing carbon emissions, optimizing energy use, or implementing circular economy practices—leaders inspire accountability across teams. Training programs that develop sustainability leadership skills are equally essential. Executives and managers should be equipped to champion sustainable practices, model eco-conscious decision-making, and motivate employees to think innovatively. Recognizing and rewarding teams for sustainability-driven achievements can further embed these values into organizational culture. Additionally, leaders must actively engage stakeholders, including suppliers and clients, in adopting sustainable initiatives. By demonstrating consistent commitment, leadership ensures sustainability becomes an enduring part of a company's identity, resulting in long-term growth and global recognition as an industry leader in environmental responsibility.

Best Practices in Promoting Sustainable Engineering Mindsets

Promoting sustainable engineering mindsets requires integrating best practices that prioritize education, communication, and practical application. Industries can start by establishing clear sustainability goals and aligning them with actionable initiatives, such as reducing energy consumption or optimizing materials. Conducting regular workshops and sustainability seminars ensures that employees remain updated on emerging technologies and best practices in the field. Furthermore, encouraging cross-disciplinary collaboration allows engineers to approach problems holistically, exploring solutions that balance economic and environmental considerations. Recognition programs—such as awards for innovation in sustainable practices—serve to motivate teams and foster a competitive yet collaborative spirit. Providing access to digital tools and resources, such as LCA software, eco-design guides, and data analytics platforms, empowers engineers to make informed decisions. Businesses can also promote a culture of continuous learning through certification programs and sustainability-focused professional development courses. By embedding sustainability into everyday practices and decision-making, organizations build a workforce that views sustainability not as a challenge but as an opportunity for growth and innovation.

Strategies for Driving Industry-Wide Adoption of Eco-Conscious Practices

Driving the adoption of eco-conscious practices across industries requires a combination of strategic leadership, incentives, and collaborative efforts. Companies must lead by example, showcasing measurable results from sustainable initiatives like reduced carbon emissions, improved resource efficiency, or closed-loop systems. Offering financial incentives, such as bonuses for sustainability-driven projects, motivates teams to prioritize eco-friendly practices. Industry-wide coalitions and associations can play a key role by sharing best practices, providing benchmarks, and facilitating collaboration between companies. Governments can further accelerate adoption by implementing supportive policies, tax incentives, and regulatory frameworks. Engaging in transparent reporting—such as sustainability audits and environmental impact disclosures—builds trust with stakeholders and showcases organizational commitment. Additionally, public awareness campaigns and educational outreach programs create momentum by highlighting the broader societal benefits of sustainable industrial practices. By aligning economic goals with environmental responsibility, industries can create a collective movement toward eco-conscious operations, ensuring a sustainable future while remaining competitive in a rapidly evolving market.

CHAPTER 16

Transition to Renewable Energy

The transition to renewable energy represents one of the most significant shifts in the modern industrial landscape, offering a solution to reduce global emissions and combat climate change. Traditional energy systems reliant on fossil fuels have been a primary driver of carbon emissions, air pollution, and environmental degradation. As global awareness of climate issues grows, businesses and governments are prioritizing renewable energy sources such as solar, wind, and hydropower. These technologies not only address environmental concerns but also present opportunities for long-term economic growth and energy security. The renewable energy transition is no longer a futuristic concept but a pressing necessity for industries aiming to remain competitive in an increasingly eco-conscious world. From technological advancements to supportive policy frameworks, the landscape for renewables is rapidly evolving. This chapter explores the importance of renewable energy, recent innovations, and the strategies businesses are using to integrate clean energy solutions into their operations. It also highlights successful case studies and future trends that will shape the global energy sector, driving it toward a sustainable future.

Importance of Renewable Energy in Reducing Global Emissions

Renewable energy plays a central role in reducing global emissions by offering a clean alternative to fossil fuels, which are the primary contributors to greenhouse gas emissions. The burning of coal, oil, and natural gas releases significant amounts of carbon dioxide (CO_2) into the atmosphere, contributing to rising global temperatures and worsening climate change. Renewable energy sources, such as solar, wind, and hydropower, produce little to no emissions during operation, making them essential for achieving global climate goals like those outlined in the Paris Agreement. By transitioning to renewables, industries can significantly reduce their carbon footprints while also minimizing environmental pollution. Additionally, renewable energy systems have become increasingly cost-competitive, making it economically viable for businesses to adopt clean energy solutions. Countries around the world are setting ambitious targets to achieve net-zero emissions by investing in large-scale renewable energy infrastructure. The importance of this shift extends beyond environmental benefits; it also enhances energy security by reducing dependency on finite fossil fuels and volatile energy markets. Businesses that lead the way in adopting renewable energy can not only meet regulatory requirements but also appeal to eco-conscious consumers and investors. The widespread implementation of renewable technologies offers a tangible path to decarbonizing industries, creating a cleaner and more sustainable future for the global economy.

Advancements in Solar, Wind, and Hydro Technologies

Advancements in renewable energy technologies, particularly solar, wind, and hydropower, have revolutionized the way industries and societies generate clean energy. Solar power has seen tremendous innovation with the development of high-efficiency photovoltaic (PV) cells, which can convert greater amounts of sunlight into electricity. Innovations such as thin-film solar panels and concentrated solar power (CSP) systems allow industries to harness solar energy even in areas with less sunlight. Wind energy, too, has evolved through the creation of larger, more efficient turbines that generate power at lower wind speeds. Offshore wind farms, built in coastal regions with steady winds, have expanded the reach and capacity of wind energy production. Meanwhile, hydropower remains a reliable and scalable renewable energy source, benefiting from technological improvements like small-scale hydroelectric systems that reduce ecological disruption. These advancements make renewable energy technologies more accessible and cost-effective, enabling businesses to integrate them into their energy portfolios. Additionally, storage technologies, such as lithium-ion batteries and grid-scale energy systems, ensure that renewable energy can be stored and utilized during periods of low production. The rapid progress in solar, wind, and hydro technologies underscores their role as viable solutions for large-scale energy transitions, empowering industries to meet sustainability targets while driving innovation and economic growth.

Business Models for Renewable Energy Integration

Integrating renewable energy into business operations requires innovative models that balance financial viability with sustainability goals. Companies are adopting a range of approaches, including direct investment in renewable infrastructure, power purchase agreements (PPAs), and collaborations with renewable energy developers. Power purchase agreements, for example, allow businesses to procure clean energy at fixed rates without the upfront capital investment required to build energy systems. This model provides long-term cost stability and aligns with corporate sustainability targets. Similarly, companies are investing in on-site renewable energy systems, such as rooftop solar panels and wind turbines, which reduce energy costs and carbon emissions. Some businesses are adopting hybrid energy systems that combine renewables with backup storage solutions to ensure energy reliability. The concept of virtual PPAs is also gaining traction, enabling companies to support renewable projects in other regions and offset their carbon footprints. Additionally, large corporations are entering into partnerships with governments and energy providers to drive renewable infrastructure development on a broader scale. These models demonstrate that renewable energy integration is not just an environmental necessity but also a strategic investment that enhances energy independence and reduces operational costs. By adopting flexible and innovative business models, industries can position themselves as leaders in sustainability while delivering tangible financial benefits.

Case Studies of Successful Renewable Energy Transitions

Several businesses around the world have successfully transitioned to renewable energy, setting inspiring examples for industries aiming to achieve similar goals. One notable case is that of **Google**, which became the first major company to match its entire global energy consumption with renewable energy purchases. By investing in large-scale wind and solar projects and entering into power purchase agreements, Google has significantly reduced its carbon footprint while supporting the expansion of clean energy infrastructure. Another example is **Apple**, which has committed to powering its operations, including its data centers, with 100% renewable energy. Apple's partnerships with solar farms and wind projects have demonstrated how large corporations can drive systemic change in energy sourcing. Similarly, smaller businesses are making strides; for instance, **Patagonia**, an outdoor clothing brand, powers its facilities with on-site solar panels and advocates for renewable energy policies. In the manufacturing sector, **Unilever** has implemented renewable energy solutions across its factories, achieving significant reductions in energy costs and emissions. These case studies highlight the feasibility and benefits of transitioning to renewables, from cost savings and improved energy efficiency to enhanced brand reputation. They also underscore the importance of collaboration between businesses, energy providers, and policymakers to accelerate the adoption of clean energy solutions worldwide.

Government Incentives and Policies Driving Renewable Adoption

Governments play a critical role in accelerating renewable energy adoption through supportive incentives, policies, and regulatory frameworks. Financial incentives such as tax credits, subsidies, and grants reduce the upfront costs of installing renewable energy systems, making them more accessible to businesses of all sizes. For example, the U.S. government's *Investment Tax Credit (ITC)* has significantly boosted solar energy adoption by providing businesses with substantial cost savings on solar projects. Similarly, feed-in tariffs and net metering policies incentivize companies to generate renewable energy by allowing them to sell excess power back to the grid. Governments are also setting ambitious renewable energy targets and mandating emissions reductions through policies like carbon pricing and renewable portfolio standards (RPS). In regions like the European Union, strong regulatory frameworks and incentives have driven significant progress in renewable energy integration. Additionally, international initiatives, such as the United Nations' Sustainable Development Goals (SDGs), encourage countries to prioritize clean energy transitions. By creating favorable conditions, governments empower businesses to invest in renewables while fostering innovation in clean energy technologies. Ultimately, well-designed policies and incentives catalyze achieving global sustainability goals, driving a shift toward cleaner and more resilient energy systems.

Future Trends in Renewable Energy Storage and Grid Technologies

The future of renewable energy lies in advancements in storage and grid technologies, which address challenges related to intermittency and energy distribution. Energy storage systems, such as lithium-ion and solid-state batteries, are becoming more efficient and affordable, enabling businesses to store renewable energy for use during periods of low production. Emerging technologies like green hydrogen storage and flow batteries offer promising solutions for large-scale energy storage, enhancing grid reliability. Smart grid technologies, equipped with artificial intelligence and machine learning capabilities, optimize energy distribution by analyzing demand patterns and integrating renewable sources efficiently. Decentralized energy systems, including microgrids, allow businesses and communities to generate and manage their energy locally, reducing dependency on centralized grids. Innovations in blockchain technology further facilitate transparent energy transactions and peer-to-peer energy trading. These advancements pave the way for a more resilient, decentralized, and sustainable energy infrastructure. As industries invest in storage and grid technologies, renewable energy will become a more reliable and scalable solution, accelerating the global transition toward cleaner energy systems.

CHAPTER 17

Smart Grids and Energy Storage

The integration of smart grids and energy storage technologies marks a significant advancement in modern energy systems, driving efficiency, sustainability, and resilience. Traditional energy grids, designed for centralized and fossil fuel-based power, struggle to meet the demands of a world increasingly reliant on renewable energy. Smart grids leverage advanced digital technologies to monitor, manage, and optimize energy distribution, ensuring seamless integration of renewable energy sources into existing systems. Energy storage, on the other hand, addresses the intermittency of renewables like solar and wind, allowing excess energy to be stored and used when production is low. Together, smart grids and energy storage form a transformative duo, enabling industries, cities, and communities to achieve energy independence, reduce carbon footprints, and improve grid stability. This chapter explores the role of smart grids in optimizing energy distribution, innovations in energy storage solutions, and the benefits of decentralized energy systems. Additionally, it highlights case studies of cities and

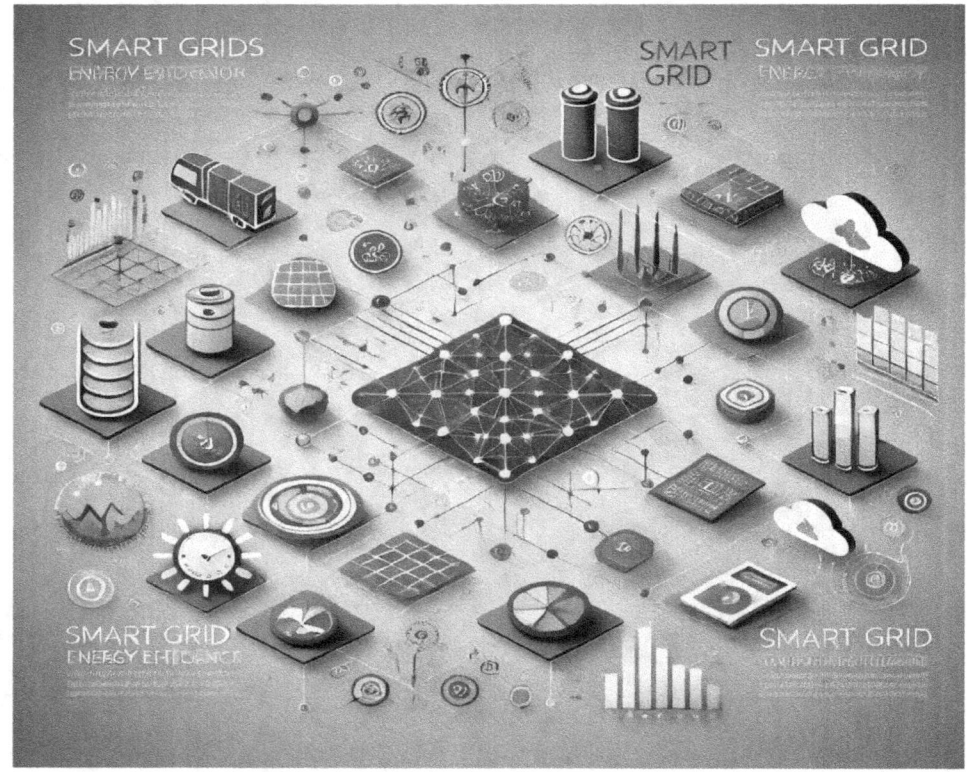

businesses successfully implementing these technologies and discusses future advancements that will shape energy infrastructure worldwide.

Role of Smart Grids in Optimizing Energy Distribution

Smart grids are revolutionizing energy distribution by leveraging digital technologies, data analytics, and automation to optimize power flow across networks. Unlike traditional grids, smart grids use sensors, smart meters, and communication systems to collect real-time data on energy consumption and production. This enables grid operators to identify inefficiencies, detect outages, and balance supply and demand more effectively. One of the primary advantages of smart grids is their ability to integrate renewable energy sources seamlessly. For instance, solar and wind power production can fluctuate due to weather conditions, but smart grids can redistribute energy from storage systems or other sources to maintain stability. Additionally, smart grids support demand-response systems, which adjust energy usage based on peak hours, reducing strain on the grid, and minimizing energy costs for consumers. The use of artificial intelligence (AI) and machine learning further enhances smart grid operations by predicting demand patterns and automating decision-making processes. These grids also improve grid reliability and resilience, reducing downtime caused by technical faults or natural disasters. By optimizing energy distribution, smart grids contribute to more efficient, sustainable, and cost-effective power systems, helping businesses and governments achieve their clean energy goals while improving the overall reliability of energy infrastructure.

Demand-Response Systems for Energy Efficiency

Demand-response systems are a cornerstone of smart grid technology, enabling energy efficiency by aligning energy consumption with supply availability. Traditional energy systems often struggle during peak demand periods, leading to overproduction, higher costs, and increased environmental impact. Demand-response systems address this challenge by incentivizing consumers—both residential and industrial—to adjust their energy usage during high-demand periods. Using advanced communication technologies and smart meters, these systems provide real-time data on energy prices and grid conditions, allowing consumers to make informed decisions about their energy use. For instance, businesses can reduce non-essential operations during peak hours or shift energy-intensive processes to off-peak times, resulting in lower costs and reduced strain on the grid. Automated demand-response solutions, powered by AI and machine learning, take this a step further by predicting energy demand and automatically adjusting energy loads to optimize efficiency. This not only enhances grid stability but also supports the integration of renewable energy sources, which may produce variable outputs. For industries, demand-response systems offer both financial and operational benefits by reducing energy costs and improving sustainability metrics. As energy systems grow more decentralized and dynamic, demand-response technology will play an increasingly vital role in creating energy-efficient and resilient infrastructure worldwide.

Innovations in Battery Storage Solutions

Energy storage is a critical component of renewable energy integration, and advancements in battery storage technologies are transforming the way energy is stored and utilized. Batteries allow industries and households to store excess energy generated during periods of high production—such as sunny or windy days—and use it when energy production is low or during peak demand. Lithium-ion batteries, the most widely used storage technology, have seen significant improvements in efficiency, cost reduction, and capacity, making them more accessible for businesses and grid-scale applications. Emerging technologies like solid-state batteries offer even greater potential, with higher energy density, faster charging, and longer lifespans compared to traditional options. Flow batteries, another innovation, provide scalable solutions for large-scale energy storage, enabling extended-duration discharge for industrial applications. These advancements have made energy storage systems more reliable, affordable, and efficient, addressing the intermittency challenges of renewable energy. For industries, investing in battery storage solutions reduces reliance on fossil fuel-based backup systems, cuts energy costs, and enhances energy independence. Moreover, integrating storage with smart grids creates a resilient energy ecosystem, where energy can be redistributed based on demand. As battery technology continues to evolve, it will play a pivotal role in enabling a clean energy future and supporting the global transition to sustainable power systems.

Benefits of Decentralized Energy Systems for Businesses

Decentralized energy systems represent a paradigm shift in energy generation and management, empowering businesses to produce and consume energy locally. Unlike traditional centralized grids, which rely on large-scale power plants, decentralized systems integrate renewable energy sources like solar panels, wind turbines, and energy storage at the point of consumption. For businesses, this localized approach offers several advantages, including energy independence, cost savings, and reduced carbon emissions. By generating power on-site, companies can mitigate the risks of energy price volatility and grid outages, ensuring uninterrupted operations. Additionally, decentralized systems support microgrids, which can operate independently or connect to the main grid, providing greater flexibility and resilience. Advances in smart technologies allow businesses to monitor and manage their energy production and usage in real time, optimizing efficiency and reducing waste. Decentralized energy also supports sustainability goals by enabling businesses to transition away from fossil fuels and adopt clean energy solutions tailored to their needs. Furthermore, excess energy generated through these systems can be stored or sold back to the grid, creating additional revenue streams. As businesses face increasing pressure to meet environmental regulations and consumer expectations, decentralized energy systems offer a scalable and practical solution for achieving energy efficiency and sustainability.

Case Studies of Cities Implementing Smart Grids

Cities around the world are leading the way in implementing smart grid technologies to create sustainable and resilient energy systems. One notable example is Amsterdam, which has embraced smart grids to optimize energy distribution and integrate renewable energy sources. By installing smart meters across residential and commercial properties, Amsterdam has enabled real-time monitoring of energy consumption, reduced waste and enhancing efficiency. Similarly, the city of San Diego has implemented smart grid solutions that support large-scale solar energy integration, ensuring grid stability even as renewable energy production fluctuates. Another successful case is Copenhagen, which uses smart grids to connect its extensive wind energy network to the city's energy infrastructure, ensuring reliable power delivery while minimizing emissions. In Yokohama, Japan, smart grid initiatives include demand-response systems and energy storage technologies that improve energy efficiency across urban areas. These cities demonstrate the transformative potential of smart grids in addressing energy challenges, reducing carbon emissions, and enhancing energy resilience. By adopting similar approaches, other urban areas can create sustainable energy systems that meet the demands of growing populations while supporting clean energy transitions. These case studies serve as powerful examples of how smart grid technology can drive innovation and progress toward a more sustainable future.

Future Advancements in Energy Storage and Grid Management

The future of energy storage and grid management is poised for groundbreaking advancements that will revolutionize the energy landscape. Next-generation storage technologies, such as solid-state batteries, green hydrogen, and flow batteries, are expected to deliver higher energy density, faster charging times, and longer lifespans, making renewable energy systems even more reliable and efficient. Additionally, advancements in AI and machine learning will enhance grid management by predicting energy demand, identifying inefficiencies, and automating decision-making processes. Blockchain technology is emerging as a tool for managing decentralized energy systems, enabling transparent and secure energy transactions between producers and consumers. Microgrid innovations will allow communities and businesses to achieve energy independence by integrating local renewable sources with storage solutions, reducing reliance on centralized grids. Another key trend is the development of smart cities, where interconnected grids, IoT devices, and renewable energy systems work seamlessly to optimize energy distribution and usage. As industries and governments invest in these future technologies, energy systems will become more resilient, scalable, and adaptable to the challenges of climate change and growing energy demands. These advancements promise to accelerate the global transition toward a sustainable energy future while improving energy accessibility, affordability, and reliability.

CHAPTER 18

Circular Economy in Energy

The concept of a circular economy in energy marks a revolutionary shift from the traditional linear "take-make-waste" energy model to a sustainable, regenerative approach. By prioritizing waste reduction, resource efficiency, and closed-loop systems, the circular economy ensures that energy resources are used optimally, recycled, and reused whenever possible. In the energy sector, this translates into innovative practices such as waste-to-energy technologies, closed-loop systems in industrial operations, and integration of advanced digital tools like AI to manage energy flows efficiently. The circular economy reduces dependency on finite resources like fossil fuels while addressing the global challenge of energy wastage. Moreover, businesses adopting circular energy practices are positioned to gain competitive advantages through cost savings, environmental compliance, and improved brand reputation. This

chapter explores the principles of circular economy practices, focusing on innovative solutions like waste-to-energy conversion, decentralized closed-loop systems, AI-driven energy management, and global policies promoting these models. Examples of businesses that have successfully implemented circular energy systems illustrate the feasibility and benefits of transitioning to this sustainable energy framework.

Principles of Circular Economy in Energy Production

The circular economy in energy production is based on a set of principles that prioritize resource efficiency, waste minimization, and system regeneration. Unlike traditional energy systems, which rely on a linear process of resource extraction, use, and disposal, circular models aim to create closed-loop systems where energy is reused, recycled, or repurposed to minimize losses. At its core, the circular economy emphasizes reducing energy waste through improved design, production, and consumption practices. For instance, energy-efficient technologies, renewable energy integration, and the use of recyclable materials in energy infrastructure ensure that resources are maximized. Businesses can adopt strategies like industrial symbiosis, where waste by-products from one process become inputs for another, reducing overall energy consumption. Moreover, circular systems often prioritize local and decentralized energy production, such as microgrids and on-site renewable solutions, to enhance efficiency and resilience. By embracing these principles, industries not only reduce their environmental impact but also achieve long-term cost savings and energy independence. The circular economy in energy production presents a forward-thinking approach that aligns economic growth with environmental sustainability, offering a practical pathway to achieve global climate goals and energy security.

Waste-to-Energy Innovations Reducing Energy Wastage

Waste-to-energy (WTE) technologies are at the forefront of circular economy innovations, offering a solution to both energy wastage and waste management challenges. WTE systems convert organic and inorganic waste materials into usable energy, such as electricity, heat, or biofuels, through processes like combustion, gasification, and anaerobic digestion. For instance, organic waste, including agricultural residues and food waste, can be processed into biogas, a renewable source of energy that reduces reliance on fossil fuels. Modern incineration plants equipped with advanced emission control systems efficiently generate power while minimizing environmental impact. Innovations in gasification technology allow for the conversion of waste into syngas, a clean energy source that can power industrial operations. Additionally, anaerobic digestion facilities break down organic matter to produce both energy and nutrient-rich biofertilizers, creating a closed-loop system that benefits multiple sectors. WTE innovations not only reduce the volume of waste in landfills but also offer a sustainable method to recover energy from materials that would otherwise be discarded. By investing in WTE technologies, industries, and governments can simultaneously address waste challenges, lower greenhouse gas emissions, and contribute to the global transition toward sustainable energy solutions.

Closed-Loop Energy Systems in Industrial Operations

Closed-loop energy systems are a key component of the circular economy, enabling industries to maximize energy efficiency and minimize waste. These systems are designed to reuse energy outputs—such as heat or electricity—within the same industrial process or transfer them to nearby operations. For instance, excess heat generated during manufacturing processes can be captured and redirected to power heating or cooling systems, reducing energy consumption and costs. Industries implementing combined heat and power (CHP) systems exemplify the closed-loop approach by simultaneously producing electricity and capturing heat for reuse. Additionally, closed-loop systems often integrate renewable energy sources like solar or wind, further enhancing their sustainability. Decentralized microgrids are another innovation, allowing industrial facilities to generate, store, and redistribute energy locally, ensuring minimal losses and improved reliability. By creating self-sustaining energy ecosystems, businesses can achieve significant reductions in their carbon footprints and energy expenses. Closed-loop systems also contribute to resilience by reducing reliance on external power grids and fossil fuels. Adopting these systems not only aligns industries with environmental goals but also enhances their operational efficiency and competitiveness in an increasingly sustainability-focused market.

Role of AI in Managing Circular Energy Models

Artificial intelligence (AI) is revolutionizing the management of circular energy systems by optimizing energy flows, predicting demand, and enhancing resource efficiency. In circular energy models, AI algorithms analyze vast amounts of real-time data to monitor energy generation, consumption, and storage, ensuring seamless integration of renewable energy sources. For example, AI-powered smart grids can detect inefficiencies and automatically adjust energy distribution, reducing waste and enhancing grid stability. Machine learning models predict energy demand patterns, allowing industries to align production schedules with peak renewable energy availability. AI also plays a role in managing waste-to-energy systems by optimizing processes like anaerobic digestion or gasification to maximize energy recovery. Additionally, predictive maintenance powered by AI ensures that energy infrastructure operates at peak efficiency, minimizing downtime and resource losses. For industrial operations, AI-driven energy management systems provide actionable insights that help businesses identify areas for improvement, achieve energy savings, and meet sustainability targets. The integration of AI in circular energy models represents a critical advancement in creating smarter, more resilient, and efficient energy systems. By harnessing AI's capabilities, industries can unlock the full potential of circular practices while contributing to a cleaner, more sustainable energy future.

Examples of Businesses Benefiting from Circular Energy Practices

Several forward-thinking businesses have successfully implemented circular energy practices, demonstrating their feasibility and benefits. One notable example is Kalundborg Symbiosis in Denmark, a pioneering industrial symbiosis project where multiple industries exchange energy, water, and waste by-products to create a closed-loop system. Excess heat from a power plant is used to supply nearby manufacturing facilities, while waste by-products are repurposed as inputs for other processes, reducing both energy costs and environmental impact. Similarly, Interface, a global flooring company, has embraced circular energy by using renewable sources to power its manufacturing plants and recycling waste materials into new products. In the food industry, Anaergia converts organic waste into biogas through anaerobic digestion, generating renewable energy while reducing landfill volumes. Another example is Tesla, which promotes circular energy through its energy storage solutions, allowing customers to store solar energy for later use and reduce dependency on fossil fuels. These businesses exemplify how circular energy practices can drive cost savings, operational efficiency, and environmental sustainability. By adopting similar models, companies across various sectors can achieve significant progress toward reducing energy waste, lowering carbon emissions, and gaining a competitive edge in a sustainability-driven economy.

Policies Promoting Circular Energy Initiatives Globally

Government policies play a critical role in promoting circular energy initiatives by creating frameworks that incentivize sustainable practices and innovation. Around the world, governments are implementing regulations, subsidies, and tax incentives to encourage businesses to adopt circular economy principles in the energy sector. For example, the European Union's *Circular Economy Action Plan* sets clear targets for resource efficiency and waste reduction while promoting renewable energy adoption. Policies like carbon pricing and extended producer responsibility (EPR) encourage industries to minimize energy waste and invest in closed-loop systems. In China, waste-to-energy facilities are supported through government incentives, aligning with the country's ambitious sustainability goals. Similarly, countries like Japan and Sweden have implemented waste management policies that prioritize energy recovery and recycling, reducing landfill reliance. Governments are also investing in research and development to advance circular energy technologies, such as smart grids and energy storage systems. By fostering collaborations between industries, policymakers, and technology providers, these policies create an enabling environment for circular energy adoption. Ultimately, global policies catalyze systemic change, ensuring businesses and economies transition to more sustainable, efficient, and resilient energy systems.

CHAPTER 19

Sustainable Farming Practices

Sustainable farming practices are fundamental for addressing the pressing challenges of soil degradation, biodiversity loss, and climate change in modern agriculture. As the global population grows, so does the demand for food, placing immense pressure on agricultural systems. Traditional farming methods, while productive, have often led to long-term environmental damage, such as soil depletion, water scarcity, and greenhouse gas emissions. In contrast, sustainable farming focuses on regenerative techniques that restore soil health, conserve resources, and maintain ecological balance. Practices such as regenerative farming, precision agriculture, and renewable energy integration not only protect the environment but also ensure food security for future generations. These approaches emphasize efficiency, innovation, and collaboration to create agricultural systems that are resilient, productive, and environmentally responsible. This chapter explores the importance of regenerative farming, the role of precision

agriculture, the shift to organic and eco-friendly pest control, and the adoption of renewable energy solutions in farming operations. Additionally, it highlights case studies of successful sustainable farms and explores future innovations that will shape the global agricultural landscape.

Importance of Regenerative Farming for Soil Health and Biodiversity

Regenerative farming is a transformative approach to agriculture that focuses on restoring and improving soil health while promoting biodiversity. Unlike conventional farming, which often depletes soil nutrients through monocropping and excessive chemical use, regenerative practices prioritize techniques such as crop rotation, no-till farming, and the use of cover crops. These methods improve soil structure, enhance its ability to retain water and increase organic matter, creating a fertile environment for healthy crops. Regenerative farming also reduces the reliance on synthetic fertilizers and pesticides, which can harm beneficial microorganisms and pollute surrounding ecosystems. By fostering soil health, regenerative agriculture encourages natural biodiversity, including earthworms, pollinators, and beneficial insects, all of which play a crucial role in sustainable food production. Livestock integration through rotational grazing further supports the soil by naturally fertilizing it and improving nutrient cycling. In addition to environmental benefits, regenerative farming increases resilience to climate change by enhancing carbon sequestration—storing carbon in the soil to reduce greenhouse gas emissions. Farmers adopting regenerative practices often experience long-term economic benefits, such as reduced input costs, improved crop yields, and healthier ecosystems. Overall, regenerative farming provides a sustainable and scalable solution for restoring soil health and fostering biodiversity while addressing the global need for food security and climate resilience.

Role of Precision Agriculture in Reducing Resource Waste

Precision agriculture is revolutionizing the farming industry by leveraging technology to optimize resource use and enhance productivity while reducing waste. At its core, precision agriculture uses data-driven tools, such as GPS-guided machinery, sensors, drones, and satellite imagery, to monitor and manage agricultural processes with unprecedented accuracy. By analyzing data on soil conditions, moisture levels, and crop health, farmers can apply inputs like water, fertilizers, and pesticides only where and when they are needed. This targeted approach minimizes resource wastage, reduces costs, and limits environmental impacts. For example, precision irrigation systems deliver water directly to the roots of plants, preventing overwatering and conserving scarce water resources. Similarly, the precision application of fertilizers and pesticides prevents runoff into nearby ecosystems, safeguarding soil and water quality. Technologies like AI and machine learning further enhance precision agriculture by predicting crop yields, optimizing planting schedules, and detecting pest infestations early. By adopting these practices, farmers can improve efficiency, increase yields, and reduce their environmental footprints. Precision agriculture not only conserves vital resources but also contributes to sustainable food production, ensuring that future generations can meet their agricultural needs. As technology continues to evolve, precision farming will play an increasingly vital role in shaping resilient and resource-efficient agricultural systems.

Transitioning to Organic Farming and Eco-Friendly Pest Control

The shift to organic farming and eco-friendly pest control is a critical step toward sustainable agriculture, offering benefits for human health, the environment, and long-term farm productivity. Organic farming eliminates the use of synthetic fertilizers, pesticides, and genetically modified organisms (GMOs) in favor of natural inputs such as compost, manure, and biofertilizers. This approach improves soil fertility, promotes biodiversity, and reduces pollution, making it a sustainable alternative to conventional farming. Eco-friendly pest control methods, such as integrated pest management (IPM), rely on natural predators, crop diversification, and botanical pesticides to manage pests without harming beneficial insects or contaminating the soil and water. For example, farmers can introduce ladybugs or parasitic wasps to control aphids naturally, reducing the need for chemical sprays. Crop rotation and companion planting are other effective techniques that disrupt pest life cycles while promoting soil health. Transitioning to organic farming requires careful planning and investment, but it delivers significant long-term rewards, including healthier produce, improved ecosystem balance, and increased consumer demand for organic food. Moreover, organic farms often demonstrate resilience to climate stressors, such as drought and extreme weather, thanks to healthier soils and reduced chemical dependency. By embracing organic farming and eco-friendly pest control, farmers can create systems that are both productive and sustainable, ensuring a cleaner, healthier food supply for the future.

Leveraging Renewable Energy in Farming Operations

The integration of renewable energy in farming operations is a game-changing strategy that reduces carbon emissions, lowers costs, and enhances energy efficiency. Traditional farming practices rely heavily on fossil fuels for machinery, irrigation, and heating, contributing to greenhouse gas emissions and environmental degradation. By adopting renewable energy solutions, such as solar panels, wind turbines, and biomass systems, farmers can generate clean, sustainable power to meet their operational needs. For example, solar panels installed on farm buildings or open fields can power irrigation systems, lighting, and machinery, reducing dependency on grid electricity. Wind energy, particularly in rural areas with consistent wind patterns, provides another reliable and cost-effective option for generating power. Biomass energy,

derived from agricultural waste such as crop residues or manure, offers a circular solution by converting waste into usable energy like biogas or biofuels. Renewable energy not only reduces operational costs but also enhances the resilience of farms against energy price volatility and supply disruptions. Governments and organizations are increasingly offering incentives, such as grants and subsidies, to support the adoption of renewable energy in agriculture. By leveraging clean energy technologies, farmers can reduce their environmental footprints, improve profitability, and contribute to a more sustainable and climate-friendly agricultural sector.

Case Studies of Farms Achieving Sustainability Goals

Several farms around the world are leading the way in sustainable agriculture, providing valuable examples of how innovation and commitment can drive environmental and economic success. For instance, Polyface Farm in Virginia, USA, has implemented regenerative farming techniques like rotational grazing and composting to improve soil health and boost productivity while reducing resource inputs. Similarly, Will Harris' White Oak Pastures, another U.S.-based farm, has successfully transitioned to a holistic farming model that integrates livestock, organic crop production, and renewable energy systems. By adopting carbon sequestration practices, the farm has turned degraded land into thriving ecosystems. In India, Amul Dairy Cooperative has leveraged biogas production from cattle manure to power its operations, demonstrating how circular energy practices can support both sustainability and profitability. In Europe, Agroecological Farm in France has embraced precision agriculture to minimize resource waste, using advanced irrigation and soil monitoring technologies. These case studies highlight the diverse strategies farms can use to achieve sustainability goals, from regenerative farming and renewable energy adoption to circular waste management. By learning from these success stories, other farmers can adopt similar practices, proving that sustainability and profitability can coexist in modern agriculture.

Future of Farming: Innovations for Global Food Security

The future of farming is being shaped by groundbreaking innovations designed to ensure global food security while addressing environmental challenges. Technologies such as vertical farming, aquaponics, and hydroponics are revolutionizing agriculture by enabling food production in urban areas with minimal land and water use. Vertical farms, for example, use stacked layers and controlled environments to grow crops year-round, significantly increasing yields per square foot while reducing resource consumption. Climate-resilient crops, developed through advanced breeding techniques and genetic research, are helping farmers combat drought, pests, and extreme weather conditions. Additionally, AI-driven analytics and IoT devices are enabling real-time monitoring of soil health, water usage, and crop performance, optimizing resource allocation for maximum efficiency. Innovations like robotics and automation are reducing labor demands while enhancing precision in planting, harvesting, and pest control. Blockchain technology is improving food traceability, ensuring transparency and sustainability in supply chains. These innovations not only address the need for increased food production to feed a growing population but also support sustainable practices that reduce agriculture's environmental impact. By embracing technological advancements, farmers can contribute to a resilient, efficient, and sustainable agricultural system capable of meeting global food demands.

CHAPTER 20

Technological Innovations in Agriculture

Technological innovations are revolutionizing agriculture, offering new solutions to enhance productivity, optimize resource use, and address global challenges like food security and climate change. As traditional farming practices face increasing pressure from environmental degradation, water scarcity, and labor shortages, advanced technologies are stepping in to transform the way food is grown, managed, and delivered. Innovations like Artificial Intelligence (AI), the Internet of Things (IoT), robotics, smart irrigation, and blockchain are reshaping agricultural operations by improving efficiency, reducing waste, and enabling data-driven decision-making. These technologies empower farmers to produce more food with fewer resources while mitigating environmental impacts. In addition, climate-resilient technologies and automation are paving the way for sustainable agricultural practices that can endure the challenges posed by global warming and population growth. This chapter delves into cutting-edge advancements in AI, IoT, smart irrigation, climate-resilient crops, robotics, and blockchain technologies, highlighting their role in creating a sustainable, efficient, and productive agricultural sector. By adopting these innovations, farmers can achieve higher yields, conserve resources, and ensure food security for future generations.

Role of AI and IoT in Optimizing Farming Efficiency

Artificial Intelligence (AI) and the Internet of Things (IoT) are transforming agriculture by optimizing processes, improving decision-making, and boosting efficiency. AI leverages data analytics and machine learning to analyze vast amounts of information, enabling farmers to predict crop yields, detect diseases early, and optimize planting and harvesting schedules. For example, AI-powered tools analyze soil quality, weather conditions, and plant health to recommend the precise amount of water, fertilizers, or pesticides needed, reducing resource wastage. IoT complements these efforts by connecting devices such as soil sensors, drones, and automated irrigation systems to provide real-time data. This interconnected network allows farmers to monitor and manage their fields remotely, ensuring that inputs are applied only where necessary.

For instance, sensors detect moisture levels and trigger smart irrigation systems to deliver water directly to areas that need it, saving water and energy. Additionally, drones equipped with AI-enabled cameras can identify pest infestations or nutrient deficiencies across vast farmland, allowing for targeted interventions. By integrating AI and IoT technologies, farmers can achieve resource efficiency, increase crop yields, and reduce costs, all while minimizing their environmental impact. These innovations are paving the way for a smarter, data-driven future in agriculture that prioritizes sustainability and productivity.

Smart Irrigation and Water Conservation Technologies

Smart irrigation technologies are addressing one of agriculture's most pressing challenges: water scarcity. Traditional irrigation methods often lead to water wastage through overwatering,

evaporation, or runoff, posing a significant burden on freshwater resources. Smart irrigation systems use advanced sensors, real-time data, and automated control mechanisms to optimize water usage, ensuring crops receive the exact amount of water they need. Soil moisture sensors, for example, monitor water levels in the soil and trigger irrigation systems only when moisture falls below critical thresholds. This minimizes overwatering and conserves water while maintaining healthy crop growth. Drip irrigation, a widely adopted smart technology, delivers water directly to plant roots, reducing evaporation and improving efficiency. In addition, satellite imagery and weather forecasting tools allow farmers to predict rainfall and adjust irrigation schedules accordingly. These technologies are particularly beneficial in arid and semi-arid regions, where water is scarce and resource conservation is crucial. By using smart irrigation, farmers can reduce water usage by up to 30-50% while maintaining or improving yields. Moreover, the integration of AI and IoT enables continuous monitoring and remote control, offering convenience and precision. Smart irrigation not only supports sustainable agriculture but also strengthens resilience against droughts and climate variability, ensuring water remains available for future generations.

Advancements in Climate-Resilient Crop Development

Climate-resilient crops are a groundbreaking solution to address the challenges posed by changing weather patterns, rising temperatures, and unpredictable rainfall. These crops are specifically developed using advanced breeding techniques, biotechnology, and genetic engineering to withstand harsh environmental conditions while maintaining productivity. For example, drought-resistant crops can thrive with minimal water, ensuring stable yields during prolonged dry spells. Heat-tolerant varieties are capable of withstanding high temperatures,

preventing yield losses in regions facing extreme heat. Additionally, crops engineered for flood resistance can survive waterlogged conditions, which are becoming increasingly common due to changing climate patterns. Innovations in biotechnology, such as CRISPR gene-editing technology, allow scientists to enhance crop traits like pest resistance, nutrient efficiency, and climate adaptability, improving both food security and sustainability. For farmers, these advancements reduce dependency on water, fertilizers, and pesticides, lowering production costs while minimizing environmental impacts. Climate-resilient crops also provide smallholder farmers in vulnerable regions with the tools to combat the adverse effects of climate change, securing their livelihoods and local food supplies. By embracing these technologies, agriculture can become more resilient to the uncertainties of climate change, ensuring global food production systems remain stable and sustainable in the coming decades.

Robotics and Automation in Sustainable Agriculture

The use of robotics and automation in agriculture is transforming traditional farming methods by improving efficiency, reducing labor demands, and promoting sustainable practices. Agricultural robots are designed to perform repetitive and labor-intensive tasks such as planting, weeding, harvesting, and sorting crops with remarkable precision. For example, autonomous tractors equipped with GPS and AI-driven systems can plant seeds and apply fertilizers with minimal human intervention, optimizing resource use and reducing wastage. Harvesting robots use advanced imaging technology to identify ripe produce, ensuring timely and efficient harvesting while minimizing crop losses. Weeding robots, powered by machine vision, can distinguish between weeds and crops, eliminating the need for chemical herbicides and promoting eco-friendly farming practices. Automation also reduces reliance on manual labor, addressing labor shortages in agriculture while improving productivity. For large-scale farms, robotic systems enhance operational efficiency by covering vast areas quickly and accurately. On smaller farms, compact and cost-effective robots help optimize processes, allowing farmers to focus on high-value tasks. By reducing resource inputs, energy consumption, and crop losses, robotics contribute to sustainable agricultural systems that are both productive and environmentally responsible. As technology advances, robotics, and automation will play an increasingly vital role in meeting the global demand for food while minimizing agriculture's environmental footprint.

Blockchain for Transparent and Sustainable Food Supply Chains

Blockchain technology is revolutionizing food supply chains by enhancing transparency, traceability, and sustainability in agriculture. Traditionally, supply chains are complex, with limited visibility across various stages, leading to inefficiencies, food waste, and unsustainable practices. Blockchain addresses these challenges by creating a decentralized and immutable digital ledger that records every transaction and process in the supply chain. From farm to fork, stakeholders—including farmers, distributors, retailers, and consumers—can access real-time data on the origin, quality, and journey of food products. For example, farmers can record details about crop production, such as inputs used, harvesting dates, and storage conditions, ensuring transparency and accountability. Consumers, in turn, can scan QR codes on packaging to verify the authenticity and sustainability of the products they purchase. Blockchain also enables traceability, which is critical for reducing food fraud, ensuring food safety, and addressing recalls efficiently. Moreover, it promotes fair trade by connecting farmers directly with buyers, eliminating middlemen, and ensuring better pricing for producers. Blockchain-driven transparency fosters trust and encourages sustainable farming practices, as businesses and consumers prioritize eco-friendly and ethically sourced products. By improving supply chain efficiency and accountability, blockchain technology plays a pivotal role in creating a more transparent, responsible, and sustainable global food system.

Emerging Trends in Vertical and Urban Farming Innovations

Vertical farming and urban agriculture are emerging as innovative solutions to address food production challenges in rapidly growing cities with limited arable land. Vertical farms use stacked layers, often housed in controlled indoor environments, to grow crops efficiently in urban settings. These farms rely on technologies such as hydroponics, aeroponics, and LED lighting to optimize plant growth while minimizing resource use. Hydroponics, for instance, eliminates the need for soil by growing crops in nutrient-rich water solutions, reducing water consumption by up to 90%. Similarly, aeroponics suspends plant roots in the air and uses misting systems to deliver nutrients, conserving water and space. Vertical farming allows year-round production, increasing yields while reducing the environmental impact of traditional agriculture. Urban farming initiatives, such as rooftop gardens and community farms, promote local food production, reducing transportation emissions and providing fresh produce to urban populations. These innovations also contribute to food security by bringing agriculture closer to consumers and encouraging self-sufficiency in cities. With advancements in automation, AI, and climate control, vertical farms are becoming more efficient and scalable. By integrating urban and vertical farming, cities can address food shortages, reduce environmental footprints, and create resilient, localized food systems that align with sustainable development goals.

CHAPTER 21

Sustainable Food Systems and Global Challenges

The development of sustainable food systems is a global imperative to address challenges such as food insecurity, climate change, and environmental degradation. Traditional food systems, while effective in meeting the demands of a growing population, have led to significant resource exploitation, greenhouse gas emissions, and food wastage. In contrast, sustainable food systems prioritize efficiency, resilience, and equity by integrating eco-friendly practices across production, processing, distribution, and consumption stages. They aim to reduce the environmental impact of food production while ensuring accessibility, affordability, and nutritional value for all. However, achieving sustainable food systems requires addressing critical global challenges, such as hunger, food waste, supply chain inefficiencies, and packaging pollution. Policies, partnerships, and innovations play a crucial role in fostering systemic change and encouraging businesses, governments, and communities to embrace sustainability. This chapter explores the key challenges of food insecurity, strategies for reducing food waste through circular practices, sustainable food supply chain innovations, the role of eco-friendly packaging, and policies driving global food system transformation. By adopting sustainable practices, stakeholders can create food systems that are productive, equitable, and resilient, ensuring a healthier planet and future for generations to come.

Challenges of Global Hunger and Food Insecurity

Global hunger and food insecurity remain critical challenges, affecting millions of people worldwide despite advancements in agricultural productivity. According to the United Nations, nearly 9% of the global population—over 700 million people—face chronic hunger, with the majority residing in developing regions. Food insecurity is exacerbated by multiple factors, including poverty, conflict, climate change, and inefficient food systems. In regions affected by political instability or economic downturns, disrupted supply chains and reduced purchasing power prevent vulnerable populations from accessing adequate nutrition. Additionally, climate change poses significant risks to food security by causing unpredictable weather patterns, extreme droughts, floods, and soil degradation, which threaten crop yields and livestock production. In Sub-Saharan Africa and South Asia, smallholder farmers, who produce much of the region's food, are particularly affected, as they often lack access to modern technologies, resilient crops, and resources to adapt to changing conditions. Addressing global hunger requires a multi-faceted approach, including investment in sustainable agricultural practices, improved food distribution networks, and initiatives that empower smallholder farmers. Technological solutions, such as climate-resilient seeds, smart irrigation systems, and data-driven agricultural planning, can play a pivotal role in improving food access and production. Furthermore, international cooperation and policies must prioritize equitable food distribution, ensuring that vulnerable populations receive adequate support. By addressing the root causes of food insecurity and promoting sustainable farming, the global community can create a future where nutritious food is accessible to all.

Reducing Food Waste Through Circular Economy Practices

Food waste is one of the most pressing issues undermining sustainable food systems, with nearly one-third of all food produced globally—approximately 1.3 billion tons—being wasted each year. This staggering amount contributes significantly to greenhouse gas emissions, resource wastage, and global hunger. Circular economy practices offer a transformative solution by emphasizing waste reduction, resource recovery, and closed-loop systems. In food production, farmers can repurpose unsellable crops or by-products as animal feed, compost, or raw materials for bioenergy production. Businesses and restaurants can adopt innovative strategies, such as portion control, inventory management, and food donation programs, to minimize food waste at the consumer level. For instance, food rescue organizations collaborate with supermarkets to collect surplus food and redistribute it to communities in need, addressing both hunger and waste. In addition, advancements in food preservation technologies, such as vacuum sealing and smart packaging, extend shelf life and reduce spoilage. Circular practices also involve converting food waste into renewable energy through anaerobic digestion and creating biogas that can power operations while minimizing landfill use. Governments play a vital role by implementing policies that incentivize waste reduction and penalize excessive wastage. Consumer education campaigns further encourage mindful consumption habits, such as proper storage, meal planning, and composting. By adopting circular economy principles, food systems can reduce their environmental footprint, conserve valuable resources, and redirect food surplus to those who need it most. These practices are essential for creating efficient, resilient food systems that align with global sustainability goals.

Developing Sustainable Food Supply Chains and Logistics

Sustainable food supply chains and logistics are critical for reducing environmental impact, improving efficiency, and ensuring equitable access to food. Traditional supply chains are often long, complex, and resource-intensive, leading to significant energy use, emissions, and food loss during transportation, storage, and processing. To address these challenges, sustainable supply chains prioritize transparency, resource optimization, and eco-friendly logistics solutions. For example, the use of renewable energy-powered transportation systems, such as electric or biofuel vehicles, reduces carbon emissions associated with food distribution. Similarly, cold chain technologies powered by solar energy can preserve perishable goods, reducing spoilage while ensuring efficient delivery in remote areas. Digital tools, such as blockchain technology, enhance supply chain transparency by tracking food from farm to fork, enabling stakeholders to identify inefficiencies, reduce waste, and verify sustainable sourcing practices. Localized supply chains, such as farm-to-table models, further support sustainability by reducing transportation distances, lowering emissions, and strengthening local economies. In addition, vertical integration—where businesses oversee multiple stages of production, processing, and distribution—can streamline operations and minimize resource use. Collaboration between governments, businesses, and logistics providers is essential to scale these solutions, particularly in regions facing food security challenges. By embracing sustainable supply chain innovations, the global food industry can optimize operations, reduce environmental harm, and ensure that nutritious food reaches consumers efficiently and responsibly.

Integrating Eco-Friendly Packaging in Food Distribution

Eco-friendly packaging is playing a pivotal role in reducing the environmental impact of food distribution while meeting growing consumer demands for sustainability. Traditional packaging materials, such as plastics and Styrofoam, are resource-intensive to produce, often non-biodegradable, and a significant source of pollution. In response, the food industry is shifting toward eco-friendly alternatives, including biodegradable, compostable, and recyclable packaging solutions. For example, plant-based packaging materials made from cornstarch, sugarcane, or bamboo decompose naturally, reducing landfill waste and pollution. Innovations like edible packaging, where food is wrapped in consumable materials, offer another exciting opportunity to eliminate waste. Reusable packaging systems, such as glass jars or returnable containers, are also gaining traction in both retail and delivery sectors, encouraging circular use. Smart packaging technologies, such as oxygen-absorbing films and moisture-regulating materials, extend food shelf life, minimizing spoilage and waste during transportation. Large food retailers and brands are increasingly adopting eco-friendly packaging to meet sustainability targets while enhancing their market appeal among environmentally conscious consumers. Governments are playing a supportive role by banning single-use plastics and introducing policies that incentivize sustainable packaging solutions. While challenges such as cost and scalability remain, ongoing research and innovations continue to drive progress. By integrating eco-friendly packaging into food distribution systems, businesses can reduce their environmental footprints while contributing to a cleaner, greener food supply chain.

Policies and Partnerships Promoting Sustainable Food Systems

Effective policies and partnerships are essential for promoting sustainable food systems on a global scale, addressing challenges such as food insecurity, environmental degradation, and resource inefficiency. Governments play a central role in driving change by implementing regulations, incentives, and programs that encourage sustainable agricultural practices and food distribution. For example, subsidies for organic farming, carbon pricing mechanisms, and policies banning excessive food waste have encouraged businesses and farmers to adopt eco-friendly practices. International initiatives, such as the United Nations' Sustainable Development Goals (SDGs), provide a global framework for reducing hunger, improving food systems, and promoting sustainable development. Public-private partnerships (PPPs) are another key driver of progress, enabling collaboration between governments, businesses, non-profits, and research institutions. These partnerships facilitate funding, innovation, and knowledge-sharing, helping smallholder farmers access modern technologies, climate-resilient crops, and sustainable farming training. Additionally, organizations like the Food and Agriculture Organization (FAO) and the World Food Programme (WFP) lead global efforts to tackle hunger and enhance food security through policy advocacy and on-ground projects. Consumer education campaigns, supported by policymakers and businesses, also play a vital role in fostering awareness of sustainable consumption practices. By aligning efforts across sectors, policies, and partnerships can transform food systems into equitable, resilient, and sustainable networks capable of meeting the challenges of a growing global population and climate change.

Case Studies of Impactful Sustainable Food Initiatives

Numerous impactful initiatives around the globe highlight the success of sustainable food systems in addressing food security, reducing environmental impact, and fostering resilience. For example, The Zero Hunger Project in Africa works with smallholder farmers to implement sustainable agricultural practices, such as crop diversification, organic farming, and water-efficient irrigation. These initiatives empower communities with training, tools, and resources to improve crop yields, combat hunger, and adapt to climate challenges. In the Netherlands, The Food Valley Initiative has become a hub of agricultural innovation, focusing on technologies like vertical farming, plant-based protein production, and eco-friendly packaging. These solutions not only address sustainability goals but also inspire global collaboration between researchers, governments, and businesses. Similarly, in India, the National Mission for Sustainable Agriculture (NMSA) promotes climate-resilient farming techniques, encouraging farmers to adopt precision irrigation, organic inputs, and renewable energy solutions to ensure long-term productivity. In Brazil, agroforestry initiatives have successfully integrated trees and crops into farming systems, restoring degraded land while providing food and income for local communities. Another success story is Too Good to Go, a European app-based initiative that connects businesses with surplus food to consumers at discounted prices, reducing food waste while addressing food affordability. These case studies demonstrate the scalability and effectiveness of sustainable food initiatives in diverse regions and contexts. By learning from these examples, governments, organizations, and businesses worldwide can adopt similar approaches to build resilient food systems that meet environmental, economic, and social goals.

Summary

The book The Future Revolution of Transforming Business Through Sustainable Innovation delves into the profound changes businesses must embrace to thrive in a world increasingly shaped by environmental and social challenges. It begins by defining sustainable innovation as the harmonious integration of economic growth with practices that prioritize the health of the planet and society. Central to this transformation is the concept of the triple bottom line—people, planet, and profit—framing a new way of thinking that balances financial success with ethical and ecological stewardship. The author explores groundbreaking ideas such as the circular economy, cradle-to-cradle design, and energy efficiency, emphasizing the urgency of aligning business practices with global imperatives like the United Nations' Sustainable Development Goals (SDGs). Sustainable innovation is not merely a strategy for survival but a means to address the pressing realities of climate change and resource depletion, unlocking avenues for growth and resilience.

In the educational sphere, the book highlights how institutions are uniquely positioned to cultivate sustainability as a core principle. By incorporating eco-friendly campus operations and weaving sustainability into curricula, educational organizations can instill the values and skills necessary for fostering a new generation of leaders equipped to tackle environmental challenges. Examples abound of schools adopting green building certifications, implementing renewable energy systems, and championing student-led sustainability initiatives, all of which underscore the pivotal role education plays in shaping a sustainable future.

The healthcare industry, a vital yet resource-intensive sector, is presented as a prime candidate for sustainable transformation. From energy-efficient infrastructure to innovative waste management practices, the book reveals how healthcare organizations can reduce their environmental footprints while improving patient outcomes. Telemedicine emerges as a powerful tool in this domain, not only enhancing accessibility but also reducing the emissions associated with travel. Furthermore, the author discusses sustainable procurement practices and partnerships with eco-conscious suppliers, demonstrating how the healthcare sector can balance ethical responsibility with operational efficiency. Addressing equity and access in healthcare innovation is another critical focus, highlighting the moral imperative to ensure that sustainable solutions benefit all segments of society.

The book's exploration of the technology sector reveals a landscape ripe with opportunities for advancing sustainability. From energy-efficient data centers to the adoption of circular economy principles in manufacturing, the tech industry is uniquely positioned to lead by example. The author showcases innovations such as AI-driven systems for optimizing energy use and waste management, illustrating how technology can act as both a tool and a catalyst for sustainability. Case studies of companies integrating renewable energy and smart city projects further illuminate the transformative potential of green technologies. These initiatives not only reduce emissions but also lay the groundwork for more efficient and resilient urban ecosystems.

In industrial engineering, the narrative shifts to the role of sustainable practices in revolutionizing production systems. Life cycle assessment (LCA), eco-design, and closed-loop manufacturing emerge as essential tools for reducing waste and optimizing resource use. The book discusses how fostering a culture of sustainability among engineers and promoting interdisciplinary collaboration can drive innovation in sustainable production systems. Examples of industries successfully integrating these practices showcase the tangible benefits, including cost savings, efficiency gains, and enhanced competitiveness.

The energy sector, however, stands at the heart of the sustainable innovation revolution. The transition to renewable energy sources such as solar, wind, and bioenergy is examined alongside advancements in energy storage and grid optimization. Smart grids, enabled by AI and other digital technologies, are presented as key to managing the complexities of renewable energy integration. The author also explores the principles of the circular economy within the energy sector, emphasizing strategies like recycling waste energy and developing closed-loop systems. Corporate partnerships and supportive government policies are identified as crucial drivers in accelerating this transformation, demonstrating how collaboration can overcome barriers to large-scale renewable adoption.

The agricultural sector explores how sustainable innovation is transforming agriculture to address global challenges such as food insecurity, climate change, and resource depletion. It emphasizes the importance of adopting regenerative farming practices to restore soil health and biodiversity, while precision agriculture leverages technology to optimize resource use and reduce waste. The shift toward organic farming and eco-friendly pest control highlights the need for healthier and environmentally conscious food production. Renewable energy integration in farming operations, such as solar and biomass systems, demonstrates how clean energy can reduce emissions and operational costs. Innovations like AI, IoT, robotics, and climate-resilient crops enhance farming efficiency, productivity, and resilience against environmental stressors. Sustainable food systems, focus on reducing food waste through circular practices, creating eco-friendly supply chains, and promoting innovations in packaging and logistics were also explored. Case studies showcase successful global initiatives that address food security and promote sustainability. By combining technology, innovation, and systemic change, the agricultural sector underscores the potential to create agricultural systems that are productive, efficient, and capable of feeding a growing population while preserving the planet for future generations.

The book concludes with a compelling argument that sustainable innovation is no longer a luxury or an ethical afterthought but a business imperative. Companies that embrace sustainability can achieve long-term economic success while contributing to a healthier planet and a more equitable society. Through the integration of these principles, businesses can secure a future that is not only prosperous but also resilient, demonstrating that innovation and sustainability are inseparable in the pursuit of progress.

Conclusion

The future of sustainable innovation is deeply intertwined with advancements in technology, shifting business practices, and the evolving demand for eco-conscious solutions. Emerging trends point towards digital transformation, the rise of renewable energy technologies, and innovations in sectors like manufacturing and agriculture as key drivers for sustainable practices. As businesses increasingly adopt sustainable product designs and eco-labeling, the role of digital technologies, including AI and IoT, will be pivotal in tracking resource use, optimizing energy efficiency, and fostering transparency in sustainability efforts. These technological advancements offer a blueprint for industries to reduce their environmental footprints and align with global sustainability goals.

To achieve these advancements, businesses must transform their core operations, embedding sustainability into every facet of their strategies. Scaling sustainable practices will require overcoming significant challenges, such as financial investment, regulatory complexities, and resistance to change. However, leadership plays a critical role in this transformation. By prioritizing sustainability at the top levels of an organization and aligning business strategies with long-term environmental goals, leaders can create resilient business models that not only drive profitability but also contribute positively to the planet. As businesses integrate sustainability into their core values, they can unlock new opportunities for innovation and growth.

Finally, business leaders must take proactive steps to lead by example in fostering ethical leadership and promoting collaborative efforts that drive global environmental impact. By setting clear, actionable sustainability goals, businesses can contribute to broader efforts aimed at sustainable development. Encouraging innovation in sustainable technologies and processes will not only meet environmental objectives but also provide companies with a competitive edge in an increasingly eco-conscious marketplace. The future of business sustainability depends on the collective actions of forward-thinking leaders who are committed to shaping a better, greener world for generations to come.

www.ingramcontent.com/pod-product-compliance
Lightning Source LLC
Chambersburg PA
CBHW082110220526
45472CB00009B/2124